CRUSH

THE HOME WINEMAKING GUIDE TO CREATING TRULY EXCELLENT VINTAGES YOU CAN FEEL PROUD TO SHARE

DAVID DUMONT

© Copyright 2023 - All rights reserved.

The content contained within this book may not be reproduced, duplicated or transmitted without direct written permission from the author or the publisher.

Under no circumstances will any blame or legal responsibility be held against the publisher, or author, for any damages, reparation, or monetary loss due to the information contained within this book, either directly or indirectly.

Legal Notice:

This book is copyright protected. It is only for personal use. You cannot amend, distribute, sell, use, quote or paraphrase any part, or the content within this book, without the consent of the author or publisher.

Disclaimer Notice:

Please note the information contained within this document is for educational and entertainment purposes only. All effort has been executed to present accurate, up to date, reliable, complete information. No warranties of any kind are declared or implied. Readers acknowledge that the author is not engaged in the rendering of legal, financial, medical or professional advice. The content within this book has been derived from various sources. Please consult a licensed professional before attempting any techniques outlined in this book.

By reading this document, the reader agrees that under no circumstances is the author responsible for any losses, direct or indirect, that are incurred as a result of the use of the information contained within this document, including, but not limited to, errors, omissions, or inaccuracies.

CONTENTS

INTRODUCTION

Wine is the most healthful and most hygienic of beverages.

— LOUIS PASTEUR

To good eating belongs good drinking.

— GERMAN PROVERB

There's nothing better than uncorking your very own homemade wine at a dinner party to the fascination and envy of your guests. You've tasted it at every stage of the process, so you know the wonderful medley of its aromas and the fine nuances of its taste. You roll it around on your palate as your guests take their first sip... "Wow, this is delicious!" someone will exclaim—and all those hours of careful selecting, harvesting, stomping, fermenting, waiting, blending, and tasting are suddenly well worth the effort.

Many home winemakers have fathers or grandfathers who introduced them to the pleasures of winemaking. If they grew their own grapes, the harvest would begin just after sunrise. Once the grapes were picked and sorted, the children would embark on a thoroughly enjoyable grape stomp, jumping into oak half-barrels and stamping on the grapes to release the juice—the first step to making great wine. Fall leaves would be sailing off the trees, the air redolent with the smell of woodsmoke from a barbecue fire—and there would even be some of the previous year's vintage to drink with the meal. Some amateur winemakers remember going into their relatives' cool, silent wine cellars to quietly sample the latest vintage on a winter's evening.

If your family doesn't have a winemaking tradition, you can pioneer this custom in yours by making wine in your garage or a suitable outbuilding using basic items found in most kitchens. Many thirsty souls took to making wine and beer in their basements during the COVID-19 pandemic—and some are still at it, perfecting their skills as they add bottles of unique blends to their wine racks, all bearing hand-crafted labels. One *New York Times* article puts the number of amateur winemakers in the US alone at around half a million, mostly on the west coast (Asimov, 2023). Some winemakers do it for fun or as an interesting hobby, while others are more serious, entering their specialist vintages into local competitions or selling them at farmers markets and festivals.

HOMEMADE WINEMAKING MYTHS

If you announce to people you know that you intend to make your own wine, you're sure to hear some skeptical responses. Below are some of the winemaking myths you might hear, together with the real facts.

Making Wine at Home Is Unsafe

Making wine at home is not much different from the way it's made at a commercial winery. As for health concerns, disease-causing bacteria usually don't survive in wine. Although spoilage bacteria might affect the taste, corrupted swill almost certainly won't make you ill. The alcohol created when sugar ferments is ethyl alcohol. Don't confuse this with methyl or wood alcohol, which is deadly. Most stories you hear about the negative effects of alcohol relate to the accidental consumption of methyl alcohol.

Homemade Wine Tastes Bad

There's absolutely no reason why your wine should be inferior to a commercial brand. Using the right equipment, ingredients, and techniques can produce a wine that's just as good—or better. You might even win an award for your efforts, and your dinner guests will certainly appreciate having a special wine to savor.

Homemade Wine Is Too Potent

Alcohol is formed when sugar is converted into alcohol. Most wines, including homemade ones, contain around 10% to 12% alcohol. Some fermented alcoholic beverages may contain as much as 20% alcohol, but this is unusual. People who make wine using berries or fruits other than grapes sometimes add too much sugar, which produces a wine with a high alcohol content. Regular fermentation won't produce wine with more than 20% alcohol anyway. You'd need to distill the beverage to reach higher alcohol concentrations (*Winemaking Facts and Myths*, n.d.).

BENEFITS OF MAKING YOUR OWN WINE

If you're reading this book, you're probably a regular wine drinker. Perhaps you're looking for a new hobby or you'd like to try your hand at making your own wines. Whatever the reason, making your own wine has several great benefits (Bryan, 2016):

- In the same way that many people drink a glass of wine as a stress reliever, you can indulge yourself in the absorbing hobby of making it yourself. This will take your mind off other difficulties you may be experiencing, as the process is straightforward. Making your own wine can also be a rewarding, enriching pastime.
- The average batch yields at least five bottles of wine, so you'll always have plenty to enjoy and share with others. Your winemaking efforts could be a great conversation starter at social occasions. You can also give your wines to others as an inimitable, distinctive gift.
- Making your own vintages is relatively inexpensive. It will cost you only a few dollars a bottle after buying your initial equipment—and you won't need too much of that either.
- Wine is not difficult to make. Brewing homemade beer often gets all the attention, but winemaking is actually much easier. The basics aren't hard to master, and once you've made a batch or two, you'll probably start trying out more complex recipes and formulas.
- Making your own wine means you get to appreciate a much wider variety of flavors and aromas than you would with store-bought wine. Because you'll be crafting endless differentiated flavor profiles, you'll never get bored.
- If friends pop around unannounced or you're invited out on short notice, you'll usually have a few bottles from your

winemaking efforts to share—or you can give one to your host or someone who has done you a favor.

- You can reuse your store-bought wine bottles for bottling your own wines. This means your winemaking will generate less waste, as you might reuse your bottles several times.
- Winemaking is tremendous fun. You'll love the process—and you can't beat the thrill of uncorking that first bottle of homemade wine.
- Contrary to popular opinion, winemaking isn't a solitary craft. You'll connect with numerous other amateur winemakers once you get started, sharing your favorite recipes and tips. Join winemaker's clubs to turn your winemaking into a shared experience.
- Your winemaking hobby will be a wonderful conversation starter. Once your friends and family know you're making your own wine, you'll be able to share your experiences with them, not to mention the fruits of your labor.
- Last, but definitely not least, you'll get to drink your own wines. The main reason you're reading this book is to get started producing your own vintages, perfect for enjoying with a delicious dinner or at a family barbecue or to warm you up while you're relaxing beside the fire on a cold winter's evening.

HOW THIS BOOK WILL HELP YOU

Whatever your reasons for wanting to make your own wine, you might be uncertain as to where to start. This book provides a comprehensive guide to making your own signature wines so you can confidently begin this absorbing and rewarding hobby. If you've been looking into the subject for some time, you might be feeling a little overwhelmed by the plethora of information available about winemaking. This book will cut to the chase, giving you all the essential information you need in a systematic, uncomplicated manner.

Reading this book will enable you to

- learn the winemaking process step-by-step.
- avoid common mistakes that might ruin your hard work.
- select the right ingredients to impart unique flavors.
- save money by making your own quality wines.
- enjoy the creative and fulfilling journey of winemaking.

I hope that this book will empower you to not only know the practical steps involved in the winemaking process but also know firsthand the excitement and fulfillment of making your own wines. You'll discover how to make wines that you'll be proud to share with relatives and friends or give as special gifts. You'll likely become part of a community of winemakers, so your hobby will become a social activity, and you'll be able to learn from others. This will make your winemaking experience rich and rewarding.

1

THE WIDE WORLD OF WINEMAKING

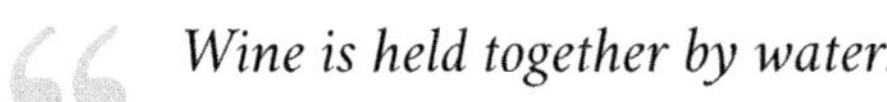

> *Wine is held together by water.*
>
> — GALILEO GALILEI

> *My only regret in life is that I didn't drink more wine.*
>
> — ERNEST HEMINGWAY

People have been making wine for centuries. Some parts of the world have a rich winemaking tradition and are still known for producing quality wines. If you thought winemaking was only for men, you'll meet some wonderful women winemakers in this chapter.

WINEMAKING'S DEEP ROOTS

These days, Europe is probably one of the best-known wine-making regions, but the practice actually originated in Eurasia, where the wild ancestors of modern grapes grew naturally between the Caspian and Mediterranean Seas. The first wines were probably produced around 9,000 years ago in China. Evidence of winemaking has been found in Neolithic sites in Iran, and it is believed that these people might have traded wine with the ancient Egyptians. Prior to this, the Egyptians made their own wines based on grapes and other Mediterranean fruits. The pharaohs thoroughly enjoyed drinking wine and placed jars of it in their tombs to take into the afterlife. The Egyptians grew their grapevines on trellises to protect them from the harsh North African sun, and they made wine in much the same way as we do today. Europeans started making wine around 7,000 years ago (Hirst, 2019).

The wild grapes native to China and Eurasia were later hybridized to produce male and female flowers on the same plants so they could self-pollinate. This meant that all the wine derived from a certain grape cultivar was more likely to be homogenous. In an interesting twist, European grapes were introduced to China around the second century B.C., as a result of the Silk Road trade route between Europe and the Far East.

European Winemaking

Phoenician traders first brought wine to Greece and its islands. Archaeological remains—including ancient grapevines, wood, and even a wine production installation—indicate that the Greeks cultivated grapes and made their own wines. They used wine medicinally and were judicious about its consumption; drunkenness was taboo. The Greeks shared their grapevines and winemaking techniques with surrounding nations, and winemaking swept across Europe and the Mediterranean. The ancient Greeks had a penchant for sweet wines, a tradition that continues, and some of the age-old cultivars are still grown and used in modern winemaking.

The Romans preferred drinking beer, and they initially didn't embrace wine in the same way as other European cultures. What little wine they produced was exported to Gaul (France), where there was a market for it. After sacking Carthage in 246 B.C., the Romans refined the art of winemaking. They classified all European grape varieties and researched which wood made the best casks. Although other Europeans corked their wine to preserve it, the Romans floated olive oil across the top. They were the first to store wine in glass bottles rather than amphorae (Wynne, n.d.).

The Romans thoroughly enjoyed their wine. They were less restrained than the Greeks, and wine fueled many drunken parties. It was used during graveside ceremonies and poured down chutes in tombs so the dead could continue enjoying it.

When the Romans conquered the rest of Europe, they brought their winemaking knowledge and vintages with them. This is how most of Europe's major wine-producing areas were established. Many produced better wine than the Romans, with Portugal in particular becoming moderately famous for the quality of its wines. By 92 A.D., so much wine was being produced outside of Rome that the incumbent emperor ordered that half of these vineyards were to be destroyed (Wynne, n.d.).

After the fall of the Roman Empire ushered in the Middle Ages, the church became the custodian of winemaking knowledge. They needed wine for Holy Communion, although they watered it down to discourage drunkenness. The French aristocracy no doubt found this tiresome and eventually joined forces with the church to make quality wines.

By 1725, Bordeaux had become synonymous with good red wine, although this official classification only occurred in 1855. The French Revolution of 1789 interrupted winemaking—and much else (Wynne, n.d.). Subsequently, vineyards became the property of ordinary people whose livelihoods depended on successful winemaking.

In the 1800s, European vineyards fell prey to numerous diseases and pests, including the dreaded phylloxera, an insect that attacked grapevine roots. The use of American rootstocks, which are immune to the insects, ultimately saved the French winemaking industry. This is why so many of the cultivars and wines we enjoy today still exist (Wynne, n.d.).

Ancient, Old-World, and New-World Wines

The world's ancient wine-producing regions include Armenia, China, Egypt, and Iran—the first places where wine was made and enjoyed. Traditional winemaking regions in Europe, the Mediterranean, and the Middle East are considered old-world wine producers. Their wines are all based on the wild grape native to the Mediterranean, *Vitis vinifera*.

New-world wines are produced in other parts of the globe—the New World. This includes Australia, Argentina, Canada, Chile, New Zealand, South Africa, and the United States (Hagan, 2020b).

In North America, the harsh climate nearly defeated historic winemakers, who struggled until the middle of the 19th century to get European grape cultivars to flourish in their new environment. The development of hybrid grape varieties, together with significant research and development, birthed the modern winemaking industry in the United States. Today, wine is primarily produced in California, Oregon, and Washington (Hirst, 2019).

The area around modern-day Cape Town, South Africa, was originally a refreshment station for ships rounding the tip of Africa on their long journeys between the Far East and Europe. The Dutch East India Company was behind the development. Jan van Riebeeck, who was responsible for setting up extensive vegetable and fruit gardens to supply ships with fresh produce, planted the country's first grape vines in 1655. Four years later, he opened the first bottle of wine produced on South African soil. Simon van der Stel, the next governor of the Cape, arrived in 1679. A passionate and experienced winemaker, he established the country's first wine farm near Groot Constantia. Its wines soon became world-renowned and are still being produced today. After the British invaded the Cape in 1795, they expanded the industry, and South African wines were exported to Europe.

As happened elsewhere, phylloxera devastated the industry. After a solution was found, the few winemakers that remained formed grower cooperatives such as KWV, which still exists. Although quality declined, the move saved the South African winemaking industry. Independent producers focused on improving viticulture and wine quality during the apartheid years, and the industry gained traction at the end of this era.

Chenin grapes do particularly well in South Africa, as they are drought resistant, and the country's Chenin wines rival those produced in France. International standard sparkling wines are produced according to classical methods (*The History of South African Wine*, 2021; *History of Wine South Africa*, n.d.).

Something Old, Something New

Vinification refers to all the processes used to create wine. Old-world techniques are still considered some of the best ways to produce wine. Grapes are harvested by hand to prevent damage, after which the leaves and stems are removed. The fruits are crushed to release their juices, and natural yeasts are added to encourage the fermentation that converts the fruit sugars into alcohol. Wines are aged, sometimes for years, in oak barrels. This creates complex flavors and ensures wine's famous longevity.

The production of champagne or sparkling wine still uses traditional methods. Champagne is created by a second fermentation process, when extra yeast is added to the wine and it ferments further in the bottle. This produces carbon dioxide, which is released when the bottle is opened and accounts for the bubbles.

There is also some interesting history attached to the wire collar that is still used today to hold the cork in place. Despite its popularity with the French monarchy and other nobles who reserved it for special occasions, champagne's tendency to explode meant that 20% to 30% of production was frequently lost (Wynne, n.d.). The monks who produced it called it "devil's wine," and they took to wearing heavy iron masks to protect themselves from exploding glass. Dom Perignon, one of the monks, was sent down to the cellars to destroy it but instead developed several techniques to rein in its explosive qualities. These included using cork collars and making the bottles with thicker glass.

In Georgia, Eastern Europe, new techniques are reproducing one of the region's ancient wines: orange or amber wine. The process uses the pre-fermentation maceration that creates complex flavors when aromatic grape varieties are used. Before fermentation, the fruit skins, seeds, and stems are added to the must for several years. Only the best quality grapes are used, and they are harvested late to increase their sugar content. This production method uses traditional clay vessels known as qvevri during this process. Grapes are crushed using modern equipment, and the juice is transferred to the qvevri to ferment. Once fermentation stops naturally, the jar is sealed with clay and sand and placed on top of a stone. Sometimes, the mixture is transferred to a new qvevri to mature, a process that lasts a few months. The wine is bottled in spring.

New-world wines often have much bolder, fruity flavors. Innovation characterizes the development of these wines. In South Africa, for example, a hybrid grape variety, Pinotage, was created by combining Pinot Noir and Cinsault (formerly Hermitage) varieties. It is often blended with Bordeaux wines to produce some of the country's top reds.

Modern winemaking is frequently based on science and technology rather than tradition. Special equipment controls the temperature, fermentation, and aging. This produces more predictable, consistent results. A new modern technique involves cold preferential maceration, where the grapes are cooled before fermentation to produce more flavors, aromas, and fruitiness.

THE GEOGRAPHY OF WINE

If you were to compare a Cabernet Sauvignon made in California with one produced in Australia, you would notice their vastly different tastes. This is because the climate, soils, flora, and even regional culture combine to create a wine unique to a certain geographical area. This is known as the wine's terroir.

Some of the main factors affecting successful vineyard cultivation and wine production include (Clemence, 2020):

- natural factors, such as climate, weather, and seasonal variations
- physical attributes, like latitude, altitude, slope, and soil type
- viticulture and vineyard management—the planting scheme of the vineyard, grape varieties, rootstocks, irrigation, and infrastructure

Many parts of the world are unsuitable for grape-growing. If conditions are too cold, grapes won't ripen, and they can become overripe in very warm temperatures. Underripe grapes produce wines with less alcohol, fresh fruit flavors, and higher acidity. Ripe grapes have high sugar levels, which have a higher alcohol content and may produce ripe or cooked fruit flavors. Optimal conditions are found at 30° to 50° latitude on either side of the equator (*How Does Geography Affect a Wine's Style?* 2021).

The location of an individual vineyard can create different climatic zones influencing the wine (*How Does Location Affect a Wine's Taste?* 2021).

- The macroclimate is the regional climate, which may be a Mediterranean climate with hot, dry summers and mild, cool winters. This delivers grapes with a higher sugar content. Certain regional climates affect the types of wine that are produced, such as Argentina's Malbec, Napa Valley's Cabernet Sauvignon, and South Africa's Pinotage. Ice wines, on the other hand, need to be picked and processed while the grapes are frozen.
- Mesoclimate refers to the location of vineyards in the same region, which includes their altitude, slope, and position relative to the sun or local bodies of water.
- Microclimates are a single row in a vineyard, which has its own unique shade and airflow characteristics.

Several vineyards are located on gentle slopes that regulate the amount of sunshine the vines receive and aid in frost prevention. In warmer climates, altitude can reduce the effects of heat. This is why grapes can be grown in the Mendoza region of Argentina, for example, where vineyards are located around 1,000 meters (3,280 feet) above sea level (*How Does Geography Affect a Wine's Style?* 2021).

Soils may regulate the climate by warming plant roots and determining how much water they take up. The ideal soils for grape cultivation are clay soils that retain water but drain well so the roots don't become waterlogged. The soil should retain heat to improve and hasten fruit ripening. Different soils contain different amounts of nutrients, which also affect the final product.

Flora in vineyards refers to the microflora—microbes present in the soil and on the fruit. Yeast is important, as it aids fermentation. There are thousands of natural yeasts, and each strain gives the wine a specific flavor and aroma. Bacteria help with secondary fermentation, affecting the end product's acidity. The interaction between natural yeasts, bacteria, and fungi might create unique flavor profiles.

The way a vineyard is tended during a particular year also affects the characteristics of that year's vintages.

Wine Regions

The 10 wine-producing countries that produce 80% of the wine made in the world today are divided into wine regions such as Bordeaux in France or Napa in California (*Explore the World's Top Wine Regions*, n.d.). Wines produced in a certain region often have a specific character, like the Sangiovese dry reds of Tuscany.

A wine region may also be determined by rules specifying things, such as the vineyard's location, grape varieties, and even the wine-making processes. These are called appellations and are used worldwide. The French AOC system is reflected on bottle labels. The United States categorizes its wine-growing areas as American Viticultural Areas (AVAs), each of which has a specific boundary with a distinct climate, terrain, and soil. AVAs don't specify what grapes may be grown or how the wine should be made.

In 2022, the top wine-producing countries in order of volume produced included (*Explore the World's Top Wine Regions*, n.d.):

1. Italy
2. France
3. Spain
4. United States
5. Australia
6. Chile
7. Argentina
8. South Africa
9. Germany
10. Portugal

The World's Top Wine-Producing Regions

Country	**Wine-Producing Regions**	**Main Wines Produced**
Old-World Wines		
France Major grapes: Merlot, Grenache, Trebbiano Toscano, Syrah, Cabernet Sauvignon, Carignan, Chardonnay, Cabernet Franc, Pinot Noir, Gamay, Sauvignon Blanc	Rhone Valley: North Rhone Valley: South	Syrah Marsanne Viognier Hermitage Comas Grenache-Syrah and Marsanne blend Chateauneuf du Pape Listrac Gigondas
	Alsace	Pinot Gris Gewurztraminer Riesling Pinot Blanc Pinot Noir
	Bordeaux	Cabernet Sauvignon Bordeaux blends Sèmillon
	Burgundy	Pinot Noir Chardonnay
	Champagne	Champagne (using Pinot Noir, Pinot Meunier, and Chardonnay grapes)
	Loire	Vouvray Chinon Muscadet Sauvignon Blanc Chenin Blanc Cabernet Franc
	Jura	Chardonnay Pinot Noir Trousseau Savagnin

	Provence	Mourvèdre Bandol Rose wines
Germany Major grapes: Riesling, Müller-Thurgau	Rheinhessen	Silvaner
	Pfalz	Pinot Noir Riesling
	Nahe	Riesling
	Mosel	Riesling
Italy Major grapes: Sangiovese, Montepulciano, Merlot, Trebbiano Toscano, Nero d'Avola, Barbera, Pinot Grigio, Prosecco, Nebbiolo	Piedmont	Barolo Barbaresco (both from Nebbiolo grapes)
	Tuscany	Bolgheri Sassicaia
	Sicily	Marsala Cabernet Sauvignon Syrah Merlot Chardonnay
Spain Major grapes: Tempranillo, Airen, Garnacha, Monastrell, Bobal	Rioja (Rioja Alta, Rioja Alavesa, Rioja Baja)	Vin Joven Gran Reserva
	Douro Valley	White Port Pink Port Tinto Douro Douro Branco

New-World Wines

United States Major grapes: Cabernet Sauvignon, Chardonnay, Merlot, Pinot Noir, Zinfandel, Sauvignon Blanc, Sparkling wine	California:	
	Napa & Sonoma	Cabernet, Pinot Noir, Sauvignon Blanc
	Lodi & Sierra Foothills	Zinfandel, Cabernet, Petite Sirah, Merlot, Chardonnay, diverse European wines
	San Luis Obispo & Santa Barbara	Chardonnay, Pinot Noir, Sangiovese
	Monterey and Paso Robles	Pinot Noir, Chardonnay, Syrah, Cabernet
	Fresno & Madera	Cabernet Sauvignon
	Mendocino & Lake	Syrah, Sangiovese, Pinot Noir, Riesling
	Oregon: Willamette Valley	Pinot Noir
	New York: Finger Lakes Long Island	Riesling Cabernet Franc Merlot Sauvignon Blanc
New Zealand Major grapes: Sauvignon Blanc, Pinot Noir, Riesling, Pinot Gris		Sauvignon Blanc Pinot Noir Riesling Pinot Gris
Argentina Major grapes: Malbec, Bonarda, Chardonnay, Cabernet Sauvignon	Mendoza	

Chile Major grapes: Cabernet Sauvignon, Chardonnay, Carménère, Merlot, Sauvignon Blanc	Cachapoal Valley	Cabernet Sauvignon Carménère
Australia Major grapes: Shiraz (Syrah), Chardonnay	Barossa Valley	Shiraz Cabernet Sauvignon
South Africa Major grapes: Chenin Blanc, Cabernet Sauvignon, Pinotage, Chardonnay	Cape Winelands	Cabernet Sauvignon Bordeaux blends

THE WORLD OF FEMALE VINTNERS

Winemaking has traditionally been a male-dominated field, and it was once rare to find women winemakers. However, all that is changing, and women are making inroads into the wine industry, managing vineyards, making wine, and blending vintages. Four women in history paved the way.

Madame Clicquot

If you drink champagne or sparkling wine, you'll recognize the name. Barbe-Nicole Clicquot probably never intended to run a champagne house, but that's what happened after her husband died in 1805 when she was 27 (*5 Pioneering Female Winemakers*, 2021). Her deceased husband left her with three businesses, but she chose to focus on champagne—a move that paid off handsomely. She called her champagne house Veuve Clicquot (Widow Clicquot) and soon became an industry leader. She developed a technique called riddling, which removes sediment from champagne bottles and is still used today. She even defied the Napoleonic blockade and exported her product to Russian nobility, a business risk that made her brand even more popular. She did all this in an age when very few women were business owners, let alone vintners.

Dona Antonia Adelaide Ferreira

The phylloxera plague almost wiped out Portugal's port wine industry—but a forward-thinking 19th-century woman saved it. Donna Ferreira inherited extensive vineyards from her family, but her spendthrift husband quickly ran through her fortune before passing away at age 33. Undeterred, Ferreira took over the management of her family's lands, caring for her workers and even fighting the government to promote Portuguese winemaking rather than importing the beverage from Spain. She traveled to England after phylloxera broke out in Portugal and used the techniques she learned to save her vineyards. She then exported her wine to England.

Louise Pommery

Widow Clicquot wasn't the only widow to produce champagne when her husband died. Louise Pommery took over her husband's champagne house when he passed away in 1860. She purchased limestone and chalk pits beneath the French city of Reims to store her champagne in a temperature-controlled environment. Then, she turned these natural cellars into a visitor attraction. She innovatively began producing sparkling white wine when the champagne industry was still in its infancy. She developed the very dry brut champagne, which proved immensely popular in Britain—it even found favor with Queen Victoria.

Isabelle Simi

In 1904 in the United States, Isabelle Simi found herself running her family's winery, which still exists today. The 18-year-old's father and uncle had died of the flu, and she was obliged to take the helm. It was no easy task, but she showed courage and fortitude. Her use of steel reinforcing in the winery prevented it from being destroyed in the 1906 San Francisco earthquake. She even kept the business going during Prohibition by producing Communion wine and selling part of her land.

In this chapter, you've discovered more about wine, including its history, geography, and the grapes that are used. Now, it's time to find out how to go about producing your own wine at home. In Chapter 2, you'll discover what tools and ingredients you'll need to get started.

2

ESSENTIAL EQUIPMENT AND INGREDIENTS

> *The discovery of a good wine is increasingly better for mankind than the discovery of a new star.*
>
> — LEONARDO DA VINCI

> *The best investment is in the tools of one's own trade.*
>
> — BENJAMIN FRANKLIN

Before delving into winemaking fundamentals, it's a good idea to take a look at the tools, utensils, and equipment you'll need. In this chapter, you'll find out not only what you need to use or purchase but also why it's needed. You will also discover what other fruits can be used for winemaking and how to source quality grapes.

CHOOSING AND PRICING YOUR EQUIPMENT

Most of the equipment you will need is easy to come by and not particularly expensive. Of course, if you decide after a while that you want to go all out with your wine production, then you might want to invest in more durable, specialized equipment.

Fermenters

Fermentation is a natural process that changes your grape juice into wine and determines your wine's quality, aroma, and flavor. It's essential to choose your fermenter carefully to deliver good results. The type of fermenter you use depends on whether you're making white or red wine. Below is a brief overview of commonly used fermenters (Clarke, 2022):

Stainless Steel Tanks

These are popular fermentation vessels used by most wineries, so you'll be in good company if you choose this option. They are available as closed-top tanks that are completely enclosed or open-top tanks. The latter have floating lids that can be adjusted for different volumes of liquid and are removable. Add a dimpled glycol cooling jacket to adjust the temperature inside the tank or wrap it in insulating foam. There are several advantages to using stainless steel tanks (Clark, 2022):

- They are suitable for any type of wine and fermentation stage and can also be used to age wines.
- They are usually available locally and can be custom designed.
- Stainless steel is an excellent choice for a fermenter, as it is oxygen resistant and not chemically reactive.

- These tanks don't need much sanitizing, and they are lightweight, durable, reliable, and easy to maintain.
- They are versatile and offer you, as the winemaker, full control over the process.

Oak Barrels

If you've ever visited a wine cellar, you'll be familiar with those huge cellars full of oak barrels. These are usually used for malolactic fermentation (MLF) and wine aging. They confer woody aromas to the wine and encourage tannin formation. To avoid having to modify the barrels or use additional equipment, you should ideally only use wooden barrels for white wine fermentation at home. Wood confers more warmth than some other materials, so fermentation will be faster. It's also recommended that you chill the juice overnight before filling the barrel. However, there are a few drawbacks to using oak barrels (Clark, 2022):

- Oak barrels are high maintenance. Wood is porous, so these barrels are difficult to clean, and there is always a risk of microbial contamination. Burning sulfur sticks regularly may help. This method involves suspending a lighted stick about halfway inside the barrel using wire or other fire-repellent materials. Loosely insert the bung and allow the stick to burn for five minutes. For a 230-liter (60-gallon) barrel, this will usually be about one-third of the stick (for 115-liter or 30-gallon barrels, divide this amount in half) (*Sulfur Stick,* n.d.). Thereafter, remove the bung and carefully remove the sulfur stick and wire. Reinsert the bung firmly. Before using the barrel again, rinse it thoroughly. Do this process once a month while the barrel is in storage.
- Wood retains pigments from the grape juice, so you might get color variations if you use the same barrel for different batches of wine.
- After two to four usage cycles, the barrels might not confer the same aromas and flavors as they did when they were new, so you might need to buy a few barrels and rotate them.
- Your reusable barrels must be washed as soon as they are drained of wine. To do this, wash the barrel with hot water heated to at least 82 °C (180 °F). Use a specialized barrel-washing tool and continue washing and rinsing the barrel until all the wine deposits have dissolved and been removed (you may need to do this several times). You can also fill the barrel with hot water and allow it to stand overnight before washing. Never use any type of soap, detergent, soda ash, or other cleaner, as this will soften the barrel and leach out the oak flavors. It's best to avoid using chlorinated or treated water for washing your barrels.

Ensure that the barrel is completely dry before storing or using sulfur sticks as detailed above.

Wood Tanks

These are somewhere between stainless steel tanks and oak barrels. You can get them with closed or open lids and add your own stainless steel accessories. These tanks are tall and cylindrical but are lined with oak staves as opposed to stainless steel. They are more economical than stainless steel and equally durable if maintained correctly. There are some disadvantages to using these tanks (Clark, 2022):

- If you are making red wine, remember that the oak will lose its ability to add aroma to your wine after being used for two to four cycles.
- The wood portion is porous, which makes sanitation difficult, and it also retains pigments.
- You'll need to hydrate the wood before using the barrel after it has been in dry storage. To do this, fill the barrel with dechlorinated water and allow it to sit for anything from 24 hours to a few days to rehydrate. This will swell the wood so any leaks are sealed. If your barrel is in long-term storage, it is advisable to rehydrate it every 90 days (*Barrel Hydration*, 2018).

Concrete Tanks

Before stainless steel tanks became popular, concrete tanks were often used for fermenting wine. Because concrete keeps temperatures stable, the fermentation process happens gradually. Micropores in the concrete create some oxidation, so the grapes' aromas will be more pronounced. Using concrete tanks does have some downsides (Clark, 2022):

- These tanks are very durable but also extremely heavy, so you won't be able to move them. You'll need to clean them where they stand.
- Concrete contains acids that might leach into the wine a little, giving it a slightly metallic flavor.
- Like wooden barrels and tanks, concrete ones retain pigments, so you'll need to use different ones for red and white wines.
- The pores are a potential breeding ground for bacteria, so your tanks will need frequent sanitization. To do this, rinse out the tank with a 3% to 8% by weight solution of peroxyacetic acid, sodium percarbonate, or baking soda and apply this with a low-pressure rotating CIP ball. Ensure that the pH is 8.0 to 8.5. Scrub with a soft bristle brush and rinse thoroughly with water. Follow the manufacturer's dilution instructions for the sanitizer used. Leave the hatches open during dry storage and rinse with tartaric acid before reuse.
- They aren't very economical and are best used by experienced winemakers with an extra budget.

Plastic Buckets

Food-grade plastic buckets with lids are a cost-effective, lightweight choice suitable for red wine fermentation. You can use anything from a 20-liter (5-gallon) bucket to a 167-liter (44-gallon) one. Some buckets come with both a lid and fermentation lock, and you can use these for both red and white wine fermentation. Make sure they are free of bisphenol-A (BPA), an industrial chemical used in plastics that has been linked to diabetes, heart conditions, obesity, and infertility. Plastic scratches easily, so you'll need to be careful when cleaning it (Clark, 2022).

Glass Carboys (Demijohns)

Glass carboys, or demijohns, are large glass bottles with narrow necks that are available in anything from 4 to 60 liters (1 to 16 gallons) (Clark, 2022). Larger ones are encased in wicker and have handles, so they are easier to move around. Usually used to transport wine, carboys make great fermenters because glass is inert and easy to clean. It's also easy to insert a rubber stopper or fermentation lock into the carboy mouth to prevent oxygenation during fermentation. You can also put them in the refrigerator for improved temperature control. They do have a few drawbacks, however: They break easily, let light in, and come only in small sizes. You can use carboys for white wine and rosé fermentation, but they aren't suitable for making red wines. If you're just starting and want to use something smaller, carboys are a good choice.

Clay Pots

If you want to make artisanal wine, then clay pots might be a good idea. They've been used for centuries to ferment wine. There are several advantages and disadvantages to using clay pots (Clark, 2022):

Advantages	Disadvantages
They are porous and let in small amounts of oxygen, so wines have concentrated flavors and textures.	Fermentation may take as much as three times longer than barrel fermentation.
They won't create any additional flavors.	The clay can harbor microorganisms, so it's important to sanitize them by washing them with dechlorinated water heated to 60 °C to 80 °C (140 °F to 175 °F).
They stabilize the internal temperature.	The pots might crack during cleaning.
There is no need for stabilizing agents or clarification chemicals.	It can be difficult to fit doors and valves.
	The small size means several will need to be used, which can make winemaking costly.
	They can be difficult to find.

Clay pots are best used by winemakers who want to focus on organic, natural production and have considered the potential drawbacks.

Fermenters in Your Kitchen

In a pinch, you could also use a large cooler filled with ice, a repurposed mini-fridge, or a freezer for your fermentation, but you will need to fit it with a temperature control device like a fermentation heater.

Other Equipment Requirements

Once you've chosen your fermenter, you will need the following (Haibach, 2017):

- A fermentation lock and stopper is fitted to the opening of your fermenter to provide a tight seal, while also allowing any fermentation gases to escape. Most wines bubble as the gas escapes. You can fill fermentation locks with vodka when not in use to avoid bacterial contamination.
- A racking cane is a J-shaped tube made from plastic or stainless steel that is used to transfer wine from one vessel to another. A small cup on the end filters out sediment. A hose attached to the other end forms a siphon.
- A bottle filler attaches to the end of the siphon. It has a small valve on the end that activates when you press the filler against the bottom of the bottle. You can purchase spring-loaded or gravity-activated valves. Bottle fillers make pouring your wine into bottles a breeze.
- Hydrometers measure sugar levels in your wine by establishing the specific gravity of the liquid. This enables you to calculate the alcohol content of your wine when it

has finished fermenting. These are essential for monitoring the progress of your fermentation.

- A Brix refractometer measures the concentration of dissolved or suspended solids within a solution. Degrees Brix (°Bx) refers to a solution's sugar content. 1 °Bx equals 1 gram (0.03 ounce) of sucrose in 100 grams (3.38 fluid ounces) of solution and represents the strength of the solution as a percentage by mass. For best results, the instrument and sample to be measured should be as close to 20 °C (68 °F) as possible (*What Is a Brix Refractometer?* 2020).
- Corkers for home use are available in two designs. One is handheld, while the other has a large lever and can be mounted on a tabletop or the floor. If you plan to make plenty of wine, then buy the mounted one, as it will be easier to use and won't leave dimples in the corks. Buy agglomerated corks, as these will fit most wine bottles.
- A wine thief is used to take small samples of your wine during fermentation to test its acidity and specific gravity or perhaps take a tiny taste. If your fermenters have a spigot, you won't need a wine thief.
- Acid test kits enable you to monitor your wine's acidity and decide whether it is to your liking or if you need to make adjustments. This is essential for ensuring that your wine tastes neither tart and sharp, nor insipid and flat.
- Non-toxic brewing sanitizer, such as Sal Soda, for cleaning your equipment, bottles, etc., helps prevent microbial contamination.
- Some other useful items you might find around your house or in your kitchen include (Dumont, 2023):

  - pieces of rope
  - masking tape

- ○ marking pen
- ○ gummed labels
- ○ food chopper
- ○ digital kitchen scale
- ○ measuring cups and spoons
- ○ food grinder
- ○ funnel
- ○ cheesecloth or similar for straining
- ○ rolling pin
- ○ long-handled cleaning brush
- ○ long-handled spoon
- ○ large saucepan
- ○ pressing bag

Specialized Ingredients

If you wish to get more technical with your winemaking, you might want to add the following to your shopping list (*Beginner's Home Wine Making Checklist,* n.d.):

- source of sulfur dioxide—potassium metabisulfite or Campden tablets
- tartaric acid when using low-acid grapes, such as those sourced from California
- calcium carbonate (chalk) or potassium bicarbonate for acidifying your wines
- potassium sorbate to inhibit fermentation in sweet wines but be sure to add enough sulfur dioxide to avoid the wine developing an odd flavor)
- packaged yeast strains (see Chapter 4 for more information on using yeasts for fermentation)
- a sulfur dioxide test kit will also be useful, in addition to your acid test kit

- clarifying agents, such as bentonite or Sparkolloid, if you don't want to wait for your wine to settle naturally
- a filter to use when bottling wine

Costs of Making Wine at Home

As mentioned previously, it doesn't cost a fortune to start making your own wine. To make 5 to 6 gallons of wine per batch, the initial supplies and equipment will set you back between $100 and $200. After that, each batch of this size will cost between $60 and $200 to make, which works out to around $2 to $7 per bottle. If you are growing your own fruit, this could reduce your costs to as little as $1 per bottle (*Winemaking Frequently Asked Questions,* n.d.). (Prices last updated in November 2023. All prices are in U.S. dollars.)

Start-Up Winemaking Budget

Prices may vary depending on where you source your supplies. The prices below provide a very general guide as to what you could expect to pay.

- 4-liter (1-gallon) glass carboy: $12
- 4-liter (1-gallon) glass carboy or wine fermenter with rubber stopper and twin bubble airlock: $15
- 34-liter (8-gallon) stainless steel fermenting tank: $300
- 24.6-liter (6.5-gallon) fermentation bucket with airlock: $30
- Fruit wine press: $60 to $111 depending on type
- 750 ml green glass Bordeaux wine bottles (box of 12): $20
- Wine corks (90 per pack): $16 to $22
- Glass hydrometer: $17
- Brix refractometer for winemaking: $19
- Digital Brix refractometer: $45

- Airlock: $3
- Auto siphon with 6 feet clear tubing: $16
- Acidity test kit for wine: $17
- Bottle filler: $6
- Winemaking starter kits: $140+ (Amazon, 2023; *8 Essential Wine Making Supplies*, 2021)

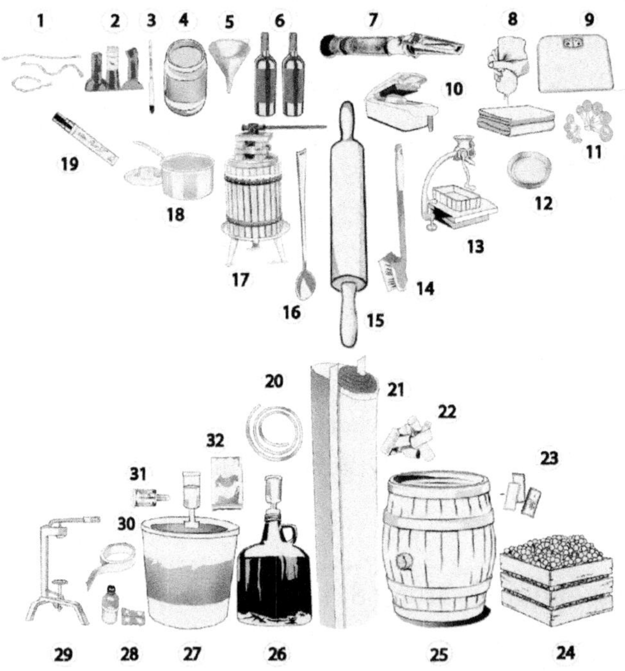

1. Pieces of Rope
2. Screw Tops
3. Hydrometer
4. Sugar Syrup
5. Funnel
6. Wine Bottles
7. Brix Refractometer
8. Straining Cloth/ Cheesecloth
9. Platform Scale
10. Food Chopper
11. Sets of measuring Cups and Spoons
12. Powdered Kitchen Gelatin
13. Food Grinder
14. Long-handled Cleaning Brush
15. Rolling Pin
16. Long Handled Spoon
17. Fruit Press
18. Large Saucepan
19. Marking Pen
20. Siphoning Unit
21. Pressing Bag
22. Corks
23. Gummed Labels
24. Wine Grapes
25. Barrel
26. Secondary Fermentor
27. Primary Fermentor
28. Campden Tablets/ Potassium metabisulfite
29. Corker Device
30. Masking Tape
31. Fermentation Lock
32. Packet of Yeast

GRAPES AND OTHER INGREDIENTS

It is preferable to grow your own grapes organically if you are planning to make your own wine—and you'll find out more about this in Chapter 10. You know what inputs you have given your vines and that they haven't been grown using harmful chemicals. However, you may not have the space or time to grow your own mini vineyard in your backyard—or perhaps you're living in an area where the climate is unsuitable for grapevine cultivation.

If you need to buy grapes for your winemaking efforts, it's essential that you obtain the best quality fruit you can afford: The better your grapes, the better your wines will be.

Sourcing Your Grapes

There are different routes you can follow to obtain grapes for winemaking (Raspuzzi, 2018):

Vineyards

If you live within driving distance of a vineyard, you might be able to buy your grapes there. Check beforehand, though, as many growers don't sell grapes in smaller quantities. If the vineyard is prepared to assist you, contact them before bud break to place your orders throughout the season. Local wineries will want to sign contracts with growers for their production, so it's wise to act early in the year. Keep following up to ensure that they don't forget about you.

If the vineyard has minimum quantity requirements, speak to other home winemakers in your area and place a bulk order. Check online for vineyards that might be selling their surplus once the season begins—you might be able to get better deals, although this is not guaranteed.

Wholesalers, Grape Brokers, and Retail Stores

If you don't want to contact vineyards, you can source grapes from wholesalers, brokers, and winemaking supply stores. Fresh or frozen grapes can often be purchased online, and the fruit is usually kept in cold storage so it doesn't spoil. Most suppliers source their grapes globally, so they nearly always have stock. This means you can make wine regardless of the season.

Ask questions about the grapes to ensure that you are getting the best quality at a reasonable price. Find out which region or vineyard they came from, what climate they were grown in, where they were harvested, and when they were shipped. If possible, inspect the grapes before purchasing to check their quality.

Many outlets also offer crushing and pressing (for white wines) services, which reduces your transportation costs. This means that you won't need to purchase this equipment straight away.

Hobby Growers

If you know other hobby winemakers or have friends who grow their own grapes, contact them to see if they are prepared to share their surplus or sell it to you.

MAKING WINE FROM OTHER FRUITS

While most wines are made using grapes, you can use other fruits, too. Some fruits you can use to make wines or fruit-based liquors include (Ando, 2022):

- apricots
- apples
- bananas
- berries (e.g., blackberry, blueberry, raspberry, strawberry)

- cherries
- dragon fruit
- elderberries
- jackfruit
- kiwifruit
- mandarin oranges
- mangoes
- melons
- oranges
- pears
- peaches
- pineapples
- plums
- pomegranates
- pumpkins
- raisins
- watermelons

Tips for Making Wine With Other Fruits

Make sure the fruit is completely ripe and has no bruises or blemishes. Rinse it off with water before crushing. Some fruits need to be diluted with water, either because they naturally have a very high sugar content or are acidic. Others, such as apples, can be used as they are.

The amount of fruit you use depends on how sweet you wish the wine to be. To make a dessert wine, you'll need to use more fruit. If you want a lighter wine, you will use less fruit. Use a Brix refractometer to monitor and adjust the sugar levels; you might need to adjust the acidity of the wine, too. Fruit acids such as malic, citric, and tartaric acid can be used for this purpose.

DIFFERENCES BETWEEN RED AND WHITE WINES

The differences between red and white wines go beyond the obvious ones of color and texture; in fact, they go back to the grapes. White grapes have a shorter growing season than red ones, so they contain less sugar and are more acidic. Red grapes take longer to ripen naturally, which allows the sugars to develop fully and lowers the fruit's acidity. This is why it's important to find out where grapes are sourced from if you are buying them for winemaking, as this can tell you whether the grapes were properly ripe when they were harvested.

White and red wines are made using different processes. For white wines, the grapes are picked and then pressed to squeeze out all the grape juice. The liquid is allowed to settle before fermentation so all the solids can be removed. Once the grape juice is clear, it is ready for fermentation.

By contrast, red grapes are picked and destemmed, but the fruit skins and seeds are retained to give the wine its red color, together with its distinctive aromas, tannins, and other components. This is known as maceration—without it, red wines wouldn't be red! This process happens in tandem with fermentation and may last for days or weeks, depending on the winemaker's goals.

As mentioned previously, fermentation converts the sugars in the grapes and grape juice into alcohol. White wines ferment at cooler temperatures than reds to ensure that their light, fruity flavors develop properly. Red wines are fermented until there are no sugars left, which creates drier wines. White wines are not usually aged, but if fermentation is done in oak barrels, additional flavors such as vanilla or tobacco might be produced.

After the maceration and fermentation processes are complete, red wines are pressed to remove the solids. They are then aged for anything from four months to several years (Eckstein, 2021). Other additives besides yeast may be added to improve or alter the flavor and texture of red wines.

White wines taste different from reds because the latter contain more tannins. Tannins are formed by the addition of grape skins and seeds to the fermentation, as well as the natural oxidation that takes place when the wine is aged in oak barrels. These processes develop the wine's flavors and aromas. Red wines often taste better after aging.

WHY USE YEAST AND SUGAR?

Yeast is a single-celled organism that belongs to the fungi family. Without it, it is impossible to produce wine, as yeast enables fermentation to take place. While some natural yeast occurs on grape skins, this is not usually sufficient to ensure predictable fermentation. However, some winemakers prefer to rely solely on this for their fermentations, especially if they want to create wines that are more representative of the area in which the grapes were grown. The wines will also differ from year to year when this is done.

Most winemakers prefer to add commercial yeasts like the Alsacian strains to their fermentations, as this is more likely to bring about good results. There are several advantages to using commercial yeasts, including (*The Role of Yeast in Winemaking*, 2023):

- a quick, reliable start to the fermentation process
- tolerating high acidity in the grapes, as well as any fungicides or molds that may be present
- even and continuous fermentation
- improved ability to ferment at lower temperatures

- being able to choose the best yeast for a specific batch of wine

Now that you know what tools, equipment, and ingredients you will need, as well as how to source your grapes if you are not growing them, it's time to start learning the steps that produce good wine. The next three chapters will provide you with an in-depth look at crushing, fermentation, and the procedure for aging your wines.

3

THE PERFECT CRUSH

> *With wine and hope, anything is possible.*
>
> — SPANISH PROVERB

> *The grape's true character is unveiled in the press.*
>
> — UNKNOWN

Crushing and pressing grapes might sound easy, but it's essential to do this correctly, as this initial step can make or break the quality of your wine. In this chapter, you'll find out precisely how to do this to ensure a quality end product.

PREPARING FOR THE SEASON

If you're just starting, you will need to set aside a dedicated place on your property for your winemaking endeavors. Crushing is usually done outdoors on a crush pad, as commercial wineries call it. Sorting and crushing can be messy, so choose an area that is easy to clean, preferably a concrete slab. Avoid using your lawn, as it's difficult to clean up, and the detritus might attract fruit flies. If possible, site your crush pad close to where you're going to be doing your fermentation.

Fermentation is done indoors, as this helps maintain stable temperatures. Set aside a cellar, garage, or even a suitable room in your house. Remember that you will need to watch the temperature during the fermentation and may need to use space heaters or tubs of water and ice to control fermentation temperatures. You'll find out more about this in Chapter 4.

Before the grape harvest begins, prepare for winemaking by checking your equipment, tools, and supplies. Ensure that your fermenters and carboys are free of scratches, cracks, and other flaws. If your equipment needs spare parts, order these well in advance. Disassemble your equipment and clean it thoroughly. This becomes more important the longer you are making your own wine, as you're more likely to skimp on cleaning by the time the season ends and you've made several batches. Clean your crush area and winery. Ensure that all areas, tables, and surfaces are properly cleaned and sanitized.

CRUSHING: EXTRACTING THE FLAVORS

The term "crush" has almost as many meanings as there are winemakers. Some use it to describe the entire process from harvesting to bottling. It's normally used to define the period from harvesting to preparing the juice for fermentation, which is when grape juice becomes wine.

Harvest time begins when the grapes start changing color, which is usually around July and August in the northern hemisphere (Wine Country Collective, 2022). This is called "veraison." The natural sugars in the grapes, which will ultimately become alcohol, increase as they ripen. Winemakers closely monitor the fruit, tasting, sampling, and measuring sugar and acidity levels (pH). The winemaker decides when the grapes have reached optimal ripeness, which depends on the desired result. Harvest time accordingly varies from year to year.

Grapes intended for sparkling wines are picked first, as they need to be more acidic, while those required for dessert wines are picked last, when their sugar levels peak. For high-quality or small-production wineries, grapes are normally picked by hand. This is more labor-intensive but means there is less chance of damaging the grapes. While larger wineries often use mechanical harvesters to save time and money, the grapes are still sorted by hand.

Depending on the wine to be produced, the winemaker decides whether to leave the stems on the grapes or not. Leaving the stems on improves the development of tannins in the wine, but not all wines require this. Grape skins shouldn't mingle with the juice when white or sparkling wines are being made, so the fruit is gently pressed to remove the skins. When making red wine, you want the skins to remain with the grapes to improve the wine's color, texture, and flavor. The grapes are crushed to withdraw the juice. This can be done the traditional way with human feet or by using mechanical crushers.

CRUSHING VERSUS PRESSING: WHAT'S THE DIFFERENCE?

Crushing and pressing are often used interchangeably in winemaking guides and books. However, they are very different processes. Bear in mind that you are not only dealing with grape juice but also with the skins, flesh, and even the stems of the grapes themselves.

Crushing is the prelude to fermentation and liberates the juice from the fruits by breaking open the skins of the grapes. The resulting mixture is called must.

Pressing involves squeezing out the must to remove the solids. This is done after a few days, usually by using a wine press, which extracts a higher volume of juice.

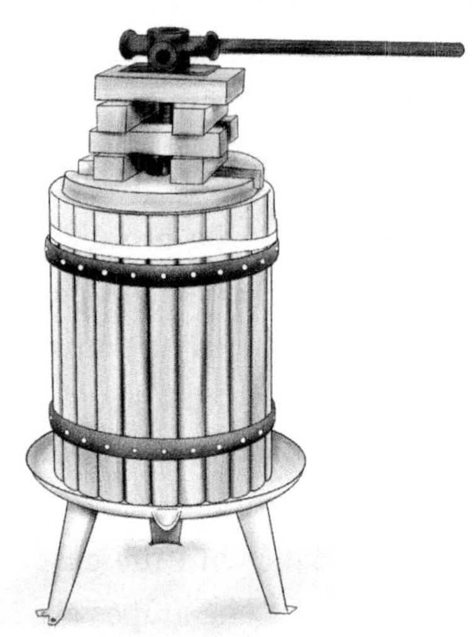

SORTING GRAPES

Before crushing and pressing your grapes, you must sort them, especially if you have grown or picked them yourself. Even if you have purchased your grapes from a supplier, you will still need to sort them, as there may be moldy clusters or inedible grapes, especially if they were grown some distance away. You will also need to remove insects and debris such as leaves. Ask other people to assist you, as many hands make light work!

For sorting, you can use a large, 2.4-meter (9-foot) folding table and cover it with a tarpaulin that is easy to clean (Shoemaker, 2020). To prevent odd grapes from escaping, erect a low, U-shaped wooden barrier around the edges of the table, securing it with clamps. Tip the grapes onto the table and sort through them in batches. Push the good grapes off the open end of the barrier into a tub.

CRUSHING GRAPES

When the juice mingles with the flesh, skins, and stems of the grapes, it creates the wonderful medley of flavors that make your wine unique. These juices will be exposed to the yeasts naturally present on the grape skins. Enough juice will be released during crushing to turn the mixture into must.

For red and rosé wines, the skins should remain in contact with the grapes during fermentation, but you don't want this to happen when you make white wine. Before you start crushing your grapes, you will therefore need to decide what wine you intend to make. This will enable you to choose whether to crush whole bunches and clusters or remove the stems beforehand. Making white wine might be more labor-intensive, as you'll need to remove the stems by hand before crushing unless you are using a destemmer-crusher.

Preparing for the Crush

Don't leave your grapes on the sorting table or crush pad for too long, as this could compromise the quality of your wine. Prepare everything the night before, ensuring that your crush pad, sorting table, utensils, and equipment are properly clean. Mix a batch of sanitizer and put it into a spray bottle, so you can give everything a quick going-over before you start.

Begin early in the morning and sort your grapes. Place the ones you will be using in a tub and tip them onto your crush pad or into the hopper of your mechanical destemmer-crusher. Clean and sanitize the area and all equipment used.

How to Crush Grapes

You can use different methods to crush your grapes, from customary foot stomping to specialized machinery.

Traditional Crushing: Foot Treading

The traditional way to crush grapes is to tread on them. While this isn't necessarily the hilarious foot-stomping party your wine-loving friends might imagine, it can still be fun, especially if you get others involved. Be prepared for the long haul, however, as grapes are surprisingly durable. It can take as long as three to four hours to crush them properly, depending on your quantities (Kraus, 2017). If you're worried about getting contaminants from people's feet in your wine, get them to wash and rinse their feet and lower legs thoroughly before starting. However, the fermentation process will remove any trace contaminants in your wine.

In larger wineries that embrace this practice, foot stompers sometimes need to jump on the grape bunches. Wineries may offer short foot stomps as visitor attractions, but a genuine one can take up to a week to complete if there are a few tons of grapes to crush. It offers a better workout than the gym, and you can expect to have some sore muscles when you're finished.

Other Ways of Crushing Grapes at Home

You can crush your grapes in a rough-and-ready manner by tipping all the grapes into a bucket and pounding them with a piece of timber, or you can use a mechanical crusher specifically designed for the job. A grape crusher normally has two rollers placed close together. The grapes are forced between the rollers to crush them. Either method works well. What you use ultimately depends on the quantity of grapes you need to process, how much work you want to do, and your budget.

Mechanical Crushers

Once you are familiar with winemaking, you might want to produce larger quantities of wine or perhaps sell some of your output. In that case, you might want to invest in the mechanical crushers used by wineries. The grapes are tipped into a hopper, where a rotating auger moves them into a destemmer-crusher.

Rollers or perforated cylinders with rapidly spinning paddles separate the grapes from the stems and filter out any debris. At the same time, they gently break the grape skins to liberate the juice. A pump then moves the must into a tank.

PRESSING YOUR GRAPES

When making wine, both the skins and flesh of the grapes need to be ruptured to release their juices. There are three zones within the fruit from which the juice needs to be extracted. These are (*Wine Bottles,* 2022):

1. the outer (peripheral) zone attached to the skin, which doesn't give up its juice easily
2. the middle (intermediate) zone, which quickly releases its juice—this is often the source of free-run juice released during crushing
3. the central zone closest to the seeds, which is also rather resistant to juice extraction

The central zone provides the most acidic juice, while the intermediate zone contains more sugars and also confers acidity. The intermediate zone produces the highest quality juice—wineries sometimes age this separately to create premium-quality wines.

After the must has been fermenting for five to seven days, you need to press it. The resulting juice will be collected in your fermenter, so the process of turning the grape juice into wine can begin (Kraus, 2017).

Types of Wine Presses

Two types of wine presses are generally used for processing grapes before fermentation (Winemaker's Academy, 2022):

1. Batch presses are used by both amateur and professional winemakers and come in different sizes. They are ideal for smaller amounts of grapes. Larger, commercial presses can handle around 1 to 5 tons of grapes at a time. Grapes are loaded in one batch.
2. Continuous presses are industrial, motorized affairs, where grapes are constantly being delivered. These can process up to 100 tons in an hour and are used by large commercial wineries.

Batch Presses

There are two types of batch presses suitable for making wine at home (Winemaker's Academy, 2022):

Basket Presses

Basket presses date back to Roman times and are still used today. Grapes are loaded into a basket formed by a ring of vertical wooden staves that are widely spaced. The juice escapes through the gaps when the grapes are pressed. The basket is first filled with grapes, after which they are covered with a wooden plate. Pressure is slowly applied to the fruit with a ratchet, so the skins are pierced and the juice released. Some winemakers add rice hulls to the grape layers to ensure that the grape skins are pierced—these do not affect the wine's flavor. Without the rice hulls, the juice will flow sluggishly, and a lot will be left behind, reducing production.

Basket presses extract the juices gently. This juice is of very high quality and contains little sediment. However, the yield from basket presses is considerably lower than that from other types of presses. It also requires a lot of manual work, as batches are smaller, and you will need to clean the press between each one.

Bladder or Pneumatic Presses

Bladder or pneumatic presses are used in smaller wineries. They either have vertical staves like those on basket presses or a cylindrical piece of sheet metal into which holes have been drilled to allow the juice to flow through. A rubber bladder in the center of the press is filled with air or water. As it expands from the center, the grape skins are forced against the outer ring. This is another gentle way to press grapes. You might think rice hulls would be a perfect way to press the grapes, but these are not used in this case, as they could pierce the bladder.

These presses apply the same amount of pressure to all the grapes. They also rotate, which releases free-run juice before the pressing even starts. They are larger than basket presses and are suitable for bigger operations. They also cost considerably more.

Other Equipment

Besides your wine press, you will need the following utensils (Shoemaker, 2020):

- food-grade buckets (at least two)
- scooper for transferring grapes to the press; you can use a 2-liter (½-gallon) water jug or stainless steel pot
- funnel and two strainers
- food-grade tubing
- primary fermenter (e.g., carboy(s), food-grade buckets, or a stainless steel tank with variable capacity)

Free-Run Versus Pressed Juice

When you first place the must in the press, the grape juice will start running out of the spout immediately, so remember to place your fermenter or another container beneath it before you start to catch the liquid. This juice is called the free run. It usually makes better quality wine than pressed juice because the latter inevitably extracts some of the tannins from the grape skins and seeds.

You can separate the free run from the pressed juice to make two different batches of wine or combine them. Many winemakers use a combination, such as 90% free-run juice and 10% pressed juice. This means that most of the wine is based on quality fruit juice, while the remaining 10% adds color, tannins, and complexity. This is part of the art of winemaking (Admin, 2012). Experiment and decide what works for you.

Pressing Grapes at Home

To get the fermented grapes into the winepress, you can usually just scoop the juice and solids out of your fermenter with a small bucket and add them to the press. If you have larger quantities, you can use a must pump, which transfers the must to the press. This can be a significant investment, although it might be worthwhile if you start producing larger quantities of wine.

When using a winepress, start by pouring the must into the collection basket. You'll then press the must to squeeze out as much juice as possible.

How to Press Must

As with crushing, do your preparations the day before, ensuring that all your utensils, tools, and equipment are properly sanitized and clean. The next day, scoop the must into the press and allow the juice to run into the receiving bucket. Continue adding must until the press basket is full. You can set aside the free-run juice if you wish and place another receiving bucket underneath the spigot.

If you have a basket press (Shoemaker, 2020):

1. Press down the must with your hands to release more free-run juice.
2. Place wooden half-circle caps over the grapes and stack the blocks until they are just above the top of the basket.
3. Thread the ratchet and spin it until it meets the blocks.
4. Insert the ratchet keys and handle before applying pressure until the juice flows.
5. As soon as this happens, stop pressing until the flow reduces or stops.
6. Repeat until the grapes are completely pressed.
7. Taste the juice frequently and stop pressing if it starts becoming too tart or acidic.

If you have a bladder press (Shoemaker, 2020):

1. Fill the basket to capacity.
2. Screw on the lid, turn on the water, and wait for the press to do its work.

If you have more than one batch of grapes, continue filling the basket and pressing until all the grapes are pressed.

Pressing Wine by Hand

If you are making wine at home, you'll probably have just a few pounds of pulp, so you can press the must by hand. Use a fermentation bag or wrap the pulp in cheesecloth and squeeze out as much juice as you can. If you are using a fermentation bucket or tank, you can hang the fermentation bag or cheesecloth over the fermenter and squeeze the juice straight into the vessel.

Carboys or clay pots have relatively small mouths compared to barrels or tanks, so you'll need to extract the juice into a large, clean jug or basin (stainless steel, glass, or porcelain are preferred over plastic, as they are non-reactive and don't contain BPA or other potentially harmful chemicals) and then pour it into the fermenter. Pressing the must by hand means you'll get a lower yield than if you use a press. Should you have larger quantities of grapes, you will certainly need a wine press to separate the juice from the must.

Now that you've discovered more about harvesting and sorting your grapes, crushing, and pressing them, it's time to get into the natural process that quietly takes place in fermenting vessels: fermentation. You'll find out how fermentation takes place, as well as the role of yeast and sugar in turning grape juice into wine.

4

HOW FERMENTATION WORKS

> *Fermentation is a dance of microorganisms, turning grapes into a symphony of flavors.*
>
> — UNKNOWN

> *You had me at Merlot.*
>
> — MY BROTHER

In this chapter, you'll discover more about the science behind fermentation, so the winemaking process is less mysterious. You'll also find out about how to work with yeast and the importance of temperature, acidity, and plenty else.

MORE THAN ALCOHOL

Fermentation converts one molecule of sugar (glucose) into two molecules of alcohol (ethanol), together with some carbon dioxide. Fermentation also produces other compounds as follows (Russell, 2019):

- Amino acids are proteins derived from nitrogen. The yeast feeds on these during fermentation.
- Anthocyanins occur in red grape skins. They create red wine's antioxidant properties and color.
- Esters are aromatic compounds that produce the floral, citrusy, and fruity notes in young wines.
- Tannins in grape skins and seeds give wines their dry, astringent texture and taste.
- Sulfites (sulfur dioxide) are produced by yeast during fermentation, enabling it to out-compete other microorganisms. Sulfites preserve the wine, although winemakers augment it after fermentation.

DIFFERENT YEASTS FOR DIFFERENT FEASTS

Several types of yeast occur naturally on grape skins, so there is a great diversity of these during the early stages of fermentation. They compete for food, creating their own special flavor and aroma profiles. However, few species of yeast can survive in alcoholic environments, so they naturally die off as the fermentation progresses and alcohol levels rise. Saccharomyces species are more tolerant of alcohol than the others, so they are often the last ones remaining toward the end of the fermentation.

Not all yeasts are good for winemaking, so wineries often use sulfites to suppress wild yeast activity before fermentation. The brew is then inoculated with a cultured yeast strain, which is often one of the Saccharomyces species. This ensures a reliable fermentation with predictable results.

You need to choose the correct yeast for making your wine. Winemaking yeasts don't impart much flavor, especially for aged wines. Light, fruity wines might have slightly yeasty undertones, creating slight flavor variations.

Winemakers use yeast to (Eisenman, n.d.-a)

- initiate and hasten the fermentation.
- improve wine color.
- determine the percentage of alcohol.
- alter the amount of foam generated during fermentation.
- reduce fermentation's inclination to stall or become "stuck."
- regulate hydrogen sulfide production.

Yeasts change the acidity of the wine, even out natural tannins, improve aromas, and activate fruit or floral esters to add flavor complexity. Some yeasts are more effective at low temperatures, while others prefer warmth. The yeast's alcohol tolerance determines the wine's ultimate alcohol content and its residual sweetness.

Yeasts are also important for wine aging or maturation. If careful sanitization processes are not followed, detrimental yeasts present in equipment, such as stainless steel tanks and oak barrels, can lead to cosmetic or flavor defects in the wine.

Home winemakers and small wineries often use just one or two types of yeast. The most popular is Prise de Mousse, which is stable and delivers good results. Preferred for Chardonnay production, it produces a dry, white wine. It is tolerant of high alcohol levels, as well as sulfur dioxide (SO_2), causes little foam, and is good for reactivating stuck fermentations.

What's in a Name?

Common names used for different winemaking yeasts can be confusing. For example, Pasteur Champagne yeast doesn't produce good sparkling wines—it's actually better to use Prise de Mousse for secondary fermentation. Manufacturers might use one name for two different strains, adding to a beginner winemaker's confusion. When ordering yeast, it's essential to provide your supplier with the following information (Eisenman, n.d.-a):

- name of the yeast
- manufacturer's name
- yeast designation number

Wine yeast is available in both liquid and powder (dry) forms. Powdered ones are easier to use, and home winemakers prefer them. They need to be rehydrated before use to avoid fermentation difficulties or poor-quality wine. This involves mixing the yeast powder with a little water or wine before adding it to the must.

Common Winemaking Yeasts

Use the chart below as a guideline when selecting yeast for your fermentation. The ones featured here are all available as dry yeasts.

Yeast Name	Temperature Range	Alcohol Tolerance	Characteristics	Which Wines?
EC-1118 Prise de Mousse	7 °C–45 °C (45 °F–95 °F)	18%	Stable Ferments quickly Low foam	Red, white, and sparkling wines
718-1122 Narbonne	15 °C–32 °C (59 °F–86 °F)	14%	Semi-dry, white wine yeast Enhances fruity flavors Adds fruity esters	Whites and rosés
BM 4x4 Red Wine	16 °C–28 °C (60 °F–82 °F)	16%	Yeast blend Dependable fermentation and improved mouthfeel Enhances tobacco, cedar, leather, and jam aromas and flavors	Red wine
D-47 White Wine	10 °C–30 °C (50 °F–86 °F)	14%	Creates full-bodied wine and enhances mouthfeel Adds ripe tropical fruit and citrus notes	White wine
ICV-K1-V1116 Montpellier White Wine	15 °C–30 °C (59 °F–86 °F)	18%	Vigorous fermenter Good varietal character	White wine and fruit wine
QA23 White Wine	15 °C–32 °C (59 °F–89 °F)	16%	Portuguese isolate Boosts fruit ethers but does not give structure to wines Creates fresh, fruity flavors	White wine

RC-212 Red Wine	15 °C–30 °C (59 °F–86 °F)	14%	Improves spicy and fruity notes and accentuates grape character Produces full-bodied wines	Red wine
Cote Des Blanc	3 °C–30 °C (55 °F–86 °F)	14%	Traditional, aromatic strain Produces fruity wines	White wine
Montrachet	12 °C–35 °C (54 °F–95 °F)	15%	Good fermenter with good alcohol tolerance Produces full-bodied wines Good for aging in oak barrels	Red and white wines
Pasteur Blanc (Champagne Blanc)	10 °C–35 °C (50 °F–95 °F)	18%	Vigorous, moderately foaming, and sulfate-tolerant Good fermenter with high alcohol tolerance	Red and white wines
Pasteur Red	17 °C–30 °C (63 °F–86 °F)	15%	Improves the development of fruit flavors and complex aromas Produces quality wines	Red wine
Premier Cuvee	10 °C–40 °C (50 °F–104 °F)	16%	Fast fermentation Neutral; good for aging in oak barrels	Red wine, sparkling wine, white wine

THE DIFFERENCE BETWEEN PRIMARY AND SECONDARY FERMENTATION

In previous chapters, you will have seen occasional references to primary and secondary fermentation. This doesn't mean that you need to ferment your wine twice. Let's start with a short description of what each one entails (Adventures in Home Brewing, n.d.):

- Primary fermentation is the first stage of fermentation. It begins when you add yeast to the must or juice. The yeast grows rapidly, and there's a lot of visible activity—you'll see the wine foaming. This is more of an organic, natural process.
- Secondary fermentation is calmer because the yeast has consumed all the sugars in the mixture and is gradually dying. As most of the alcohol has already been produced, the yeast will struggle to survive. Secondary fermentation normally continues for no more than two weeks at the most—it is simply the second stage of fermentation. This is when the chemical reactions occur that will ultimately create the wine's unique characteristics, body, aromas, and flavors. It's also when winemakers add certain chemicals to achieve various winemaking goals during the process, such as pH regulation or improved shelf life.

The Excitement of Primary Fermentation

Primary fermentation is vigorous and relatively quick. It usually lasts for around three to five days, although it could take as long as seven days to complete. Around 70% of fermentation activity takes place during that time, and the must or juice produces copious amounts of foam. During primary fermentation, the vessel should be open to the air to oxygenate the mixture. The number of yeast cells will multiply by up to 100 or 200 times at this stage. This is why the airlock should not be used during primary fermentation—unless you enjoy witnessing grape juice explosions (Adventures in Home Brewing, n.d.)!

The yeast consumes the sugars in the must very rapidly. Although alcohol is produced, the yeast is mainly concerned with reproducing itself. As fermentation progresses, the sugar and yeast nutrients diminish and alcohol starts to form. This slows fermentation down.

There is no specific dividing line between primary and secondary fermentation. Primary fermentation is generally considered to be over once the wine's specific gravity has dropped below 1.030 or when it is ready to be racked into the secondary fermenter. (Adventures in Home Brewing, n.d.).

Managing Primary Fermentation

Most winemakers leave the lid off the fermenter during the primary stage of fermentation, as the yeast needs oxygen to replicate and do its work. It is recommended that you use mesh or a similar covering to prevent insects from getting into your ferment. You should stir the mixture gently on occasion during this fermentation stage, as this helps to resuspend the yeast and mix in any grape skins or other solids that might still be present.

It is common practice to leave the fermentation airlock off your fermenter during primary fermentation. If the process starts well and ferments vigorously, producing plenty of carbon dioxide—this is why it foams or bubbles—then there is little chance that your wine will become compromised. Remember that the carbon dioxide gas is rising fast from the ferment, protecting it from any airborne nasties. The fast action of the yeast will also destroy any contaminants that find their way into your must.

If you are still concerned about contamination, you can leave the fermenter lid on with the airlock in place. This means that your ferment will be better protected, but it will proceed at a significantly slower pace. Either way, you will still get wine.

Once the fermentation slows and you rack your wine before transferring it to a second fermenting vessel, you must close the second fermenter and have an airlock in place. From now on, you'll need to be careful about oxidation (this will be discussed later in this chapter). The ferment will be much calmer and proceed at a slower pace.

Building Character: The Second Fermentation

Secondary fermentation starts when you transfer your wine out of the primary fermenter into another container, such as a glass carboy or oak barrel for bulk aging. By this time, the foaming and bubbling will have reduced significantly, so it's unlikely that it will foam out of the secondary fermentation vessel. You will also need to degas the mixture and use racking to remove sediment and solids. Find a cool place with a stable air temperature for this part of the fermentation.

Don't wait too long to do secondary fermentation. The wine needs to be removed from the dead yeast cells (lees), which form sediment in the fermenter, in a timely fashion. If this is not done, the live yeast cells will feed on the dead ones when the yeast runs out of sugars to consume. This makes the wine taste bitter or metallic. Experienced winemakers sometimes leave the lees in for slightly longer, as this results in a creamy, buttery-tasting wine.

Ensure that your fermentation vessels are filled to the brim to avoid excess oxygen getting into your wine. If your container is too large for the amount of wine you have, you can top it off with argon gas—an inert atmospheric gas that is extracted and used for industrial and other processes—or another similar wine, add glass marbles to take up the space, or use a smaller container.

MALOLACTIC FERMENTATION (MLF)

Malolactic fermentation (MLF) is responsible for the creamy, buttery flavors found in some white and red wines. It takes place once the alcoholic fermentation has completed. This type of fermentation doesn't involve yeast. Instead, the wine is inoculated with a bacterium called Oenococcus oeni, which converts tart-tasting malic acid to lactic acid, which is the same acid found in milk. MLF therefore reduces the acidity in the wine while also releasing some carbon dioxide.

MLF bacteria are often present in oak barrels, so red wines tend to undergo MLF simultaneously when aged in these barrels. Winemakers usually only allow a small percentage of their white wines to experience MLF. This adds body and texture while retaining the floral and citrussy aromas that are classic signs of oak-aged white wines.

MLF has the following benefits for winemakers (*A Basic Guide to Malolactic Fermentation*, 2021):

- It lowers the acidity of the wine because malic acid is stronger than lactic acid. However, the reduction in acidity can make wines vulnerable to spoilage, so some winemakers add tartaric acid after MLF to raise the acidity again.
- Removing malic acid stabilizes red wines microbiologically, as malic acid provides a nutrient source for unwanted yeasts and bacteria, which can result in spoilage, bubbliness, and poor flavors.
- MLF replaces tart, fruity flavors with buttery, mellow ones, which creates softer wines with a smooth, full-bodied mouthfeel.

- If MLF takes place before bottling, this decreases the likelihood that MLF will occur in the bottle, thereby increasing the stability of the wine. Wine can turn cloudy and slightly bubbly if MLF takes place in the bottle.

Most red wines and about a fifth of white wines undergo MLF, which is very often initiated by winemakers because of its benefits. Dry white wines such as Chardonnay and Cabernet Sauvignon are more suitable for MLF fermentation, while sweeter Rieslings and Gewürztraminer are less so. MLF tends to occur in cooler climates, such as Burgundy and Champagne, where low temperatures make for more acidic grapes.

Ensuring Successful MLF

If you wish to stimulate MLF by inoculating your wine with Oenococcus oeni bacteria, you need to ensure that the wine is at the right temperature and has the right pH, alcohol level, and sulfuric acid concentration. If any of these factors become less favorable, MLF will be more difficult to achieve. Below is a brief guide for encouraging MLF (*Fact Sheet,* 2020):

- The temperature of the wine should be between 18 °C and 22 °C (64.4 °F and 71.6 °F) and not lower than 16 °C (60.8 °F) or over 25 °C (77 °F).
- When pH is very low, molecular sulfur dioxide concentrations will be higher, which can create toxic conditions for MLF bacteria. The ideal pH for MLF should therefore be 3.3 to 3.5.
- MLF is very sensitive to molecular sulfur dioxide. It is recommended that wine intended for MLF does not contain any free or molecular sulfur dioxide. Sulfur

dioxide concentrations should be lower than 30 milligrams per liter (0.0040 ounces per gallon).
- Alcohol levels should be less than 13% alcohol per volume for MLF. If alcohol levels are over 15%, it is recommended that an alcohol-tolerant strain of MLF bacteria be used.
- Other inhibitory factors may include high residual copper or fungicide levels from the vineyard.

Preparing for MLF

Ensure that the yeast-driven, alcoholic fermentation of your wine has stopped completely before inoculating the wine with MLF bacteria. Freeze-dried MLF bacteria are available in sachets. Ensure that you adhere to the manufacturer's instructions when preparing the culture before adding it to your wine. If sachets are labeled "direct addition," then the contents can be added to the wine as is. Some manufacturers may require the culture to be hydrated before use and will give directions as to how this should be done. Once hydrated, the culture is then added to the wine and stirred in thoroughly.

When MLF Completes

Continue the fermentation until malic acid is no longer detected or at extremely low levels (0.1 gram per liter or less). You will find that the pH level of the wine will drop after MLF, which means that the total acidity (TA) will be around half what it was prior to MLF (*Fact Sheet*, 2020).

Preventing MLF

Some winemakers prefer not to allow their wines to undergo MLF. This is usually the case in warmer regions, where grapes and wines are less acidic. MLF will occur only when temperatures are over 20 °C (68 °F). Keeping wine below this temperature will, therefore, help to prevent MLF. Racking wines early will also prevent MLF, as this usually lowers the pH. MLF won't take place if the wine's pH is below 3.1. Sulfur dioxide can also be added to the wine, as this kills off lactic acid bacteria. Some winemakers also filter out lactic acid bacteria once the wine has finished fermenting to prevent spontaneous MLF from taking place in the bottles (*A Basic Guide to Malolactic Fermentation*, 2021).

NATURAL FERMENTATION

Also called spontaneous fermentation, natural or uninoculated fermentations occur when only the natural yeasts present on the grape skins are used for fermentation. Factors such as fruit maturity, vineyard location and age, the use of antifungal agents, and harvesting techniques can all affect the density and type of yeasts present. Studies indicate that, in at least some cases, around 68% of the natural yeasts present in vineyards are sufficient to begin the fermentation process after crushing (Hakim, 2018).

However, not all of them survive. Temperature and acidity affect the types of yeast present and their persistence. Certain yeasts are sensitive to the sulfites added by winemakers. When the fermentation is inoculated with Saccharomyces yeasts, they become dominant.

SELECTING YEAST

When selecting a yeast strain, ensure that it is suitable for the grape variety you are using, together with the desired wine style (i.e., dry, full-bodied, or sweet). Consider variables such as temperature, acidity, and any other conditions that could negatively affect the yeast. Winemakers, especially beginners, often opt for a generic yeast without examining its properties and suitability.

Below is a summary of considerations for winemaking yeasts (Pambianchi, 2019):

Wine Type

Specific yeast strains enable the grape varieties to reach their full potential in your wine. A white wine yeast, for example, might improve fruitiness, while a red wine yeast might reinforce color or texture. Certain yeast strains may help to improve MLF or restart a stuck fermentation.

Temperature

Fermentation temperatures must remain within the recommended range for the yeast strain you are using to remain effective. If temperatures deviate from this, the yeast may become inactive, resulting in a stuck fermentation. Yeasts that tolerate lower temperatures are recommended for white wines. Red wine fermentations generate heat, so a yeast tolerant of higher temperatures may be required. High temperatures may result in the creation of undesirable esters, however. These may create synthetically unpleasant off-flavors and aromas, such as nail polish, solvents, or formalin.

Alcohol Tolerance

Different yeast strains have different alcohol tolerances. When high alcohol levels are required during the making of Port-style wines, for instance, using a yeast with low alcohol tolerance might deactivate fermentation. While some yeast strains can tolerate alcohol levels of 14% to 18% alcohol per volume, this is not always the case.

Rate of Fermentation

White wines require slower fermentation than red wines, but the latter should nevertheless ferment steadily. If fermentation happens too fast, hydrogen sulfide might develop in the wine, creating rotten-egg or burned-rubber aromas and tastes. The higher the temperature, the faster the fermentation, so consider the ambient temperature of your fermentation area when selecting a yeast strain. If temperatures are too high for the strain selected, the yeast will become stressed, compromising your results.

Foam Production

This is a natural part of fermentation. If you choose a yeast strain more inclined to generate foam, ensure that your fermentation vessel has sufficient capacity to hold the extra volume. Your fermentation vessels should be filled only three-quarters to allow for expansion and foaming during fermentation.

Flocculation

This is the tendency of yeast to settle out after fermentation and drift to the bottom of the fermenter, where it forms sediment. In early-drinking wines, sedimentation needs to happen quickly, so the wine can be clarified and bottled earlier. A certain amount of wine will usually be lost, depending on how much spent yeast collects at the bottom of the fermenter. Don't worry, as this is all part of the fermentation process.

Volatile Acid (VA) and Acetaldehyde Formation

Small concentrations of acetic acid, volatile acidity (VA), and acetaldehyde noticeably impact the bouquet of your wine. At higher concentrations, they can negatively affect wine quality and shelf life. Choose a yeast strain that won't produce VA and minimizes acetaldehyde production.

Ester Production

Matching the yeast strain to the grape varieties you are using will promote the formation of esters and other compounds that create your wine's unique aromas and flavors.

Sulfur Dioxide (SO_2) Production

This is a natural byproduct of fermentation. If you are using bacteria to stimulate MLF and sulfur dioxide levels rise above the bacteria's tolerance threshold, this could inhibit MLF, especially if you added sulfur when you began your fermentation. If you wish to use MLF, choose a yeast that produces very little sulfur dioxide.

Yeast Nutrients

Yeast needs nourishment while it is working in your fermenter. Grapes from a poor vintage or that were affected by rain or gray rot will have insufficient nutrients to support the yeast. Some yeasts need more nutrients when they are working in adverse conditions.

Nitrogen is an essential grape nutrient that encourages yeast growth and ensures successful fermentation, good wine aromas and tastes, and the achievement of the right wine style. Therefore, knowing the yeast available nitrogen (YAN) content of the must before fermentation is important. Different yeasts have different nitrogen requirements. If insufficient nitrogen is present, this can lead to sluggish or even stuck fermentations. A YAN analysis will tell you how much nitrogen is in your grapes, must, and juice. The minimum YAN requirements for low-risk fermentations are 150 milligrams per liter for white wines and 100 milligrams per liter for red wines. Maximum YAN demands are usually between 330 and 400 milligrams per liter (AWRI, 2023).

FERMENTATION TEMPERATURE

The speed and efficiency of fermentation depend on the temperature. Heat will create a faster fermentation, but the wine might taste unpleasant. The action of the yeast generates heat, even in cool environments, so you need to monitor fermentation temperatures constantly. Invest in a good-quality thermometer and calibrate it to ensure its accuracy.

Ideal temperatures for fermenting red wines are generally between 20 °C and 30 °C (70 °F and 85 °F). This provides more tannins and better color. Fruity flavors and aromas will disappear, which is good for red wines. When temperatures reach around 32 °C (90 °F), you are entering the danger zone (*Effects of Fermentation Temperature*, 2013).

White wine fermentation temperatures are much cooler, averaging between 7 °C and 16 °C (45 °F and 60 °F). This preserves the aromas and fruitiness, which is desirable in white wines. White wine ferments take considerably longer—at lower temperatures, they might take a few months (*Effects of Fermentation Temperature*, 2013).

Air temperatures may indirectly affect fermentation results. Air can be a heat source or sink, depending on the season, and this can cause fluctuations in fermentation temperatures. Cold weather reduces yeast's activity, as the cells clump together and separate from the liquid. This slows the process.

To take the temperature of your ferment, open the fermenter and slip in your sanitized thermometer. Don't leave the vessel open long to minimize the amount of oxygen that reaches the liquid. You can also use a self-adhesive temperature strip that can be attached to the outside of buckets or carboys, so you can get a reading without opening the fermenter.

Regulating Fermentation Temperatures

If your ferment starts cooling down excessively, use an insulating wrap. This low-tech option traps the heat the fermentation is producing. You can also wrap your fermenter in an electrical heating belt or stand it on a heating pad.

To cool a hot ferment, place the fermenter in an ice bath. Put it into a large plastic tub, add cold water and ice, and leave it there until it reaches the desired temperature. For larger tanks, use a stainless steel tubing coil or heat exchanger and run cold water through it. This works slowly, and you might need to do a little DIY with a garden pump to circulate cold water through the system. Be careful not to cool the mixture too much or the fermentation might slow down or stop.

WINE ACIDITY AND PH

Determining the acidity and pH of wine is important because both impact the quality of the final product. Wine acidity helps with stability and preservation, while pH is a measure of acidity and alkalinity that indicates the number of hydrogen ions present. It is calibrated on a scale from 0 to 14. Readings below 7.0 are acidic, while ones above 7.0 are alkaline. Neutral pH is between 6 and 7. It's a logarithmic scale, which means that a single point lower on the pH scale is actually around 10 times more acidic (O'Donnell, 2022).

Wine acidity is measured as pH and total acidity (TA), the latter of which is calculated in grams per liter. Most winemakers prefer to only use pH values to calculate wine acidity, as this determines microbial stability. Wine contains lactic, malic, and tartaric acids. The latter is the strongest, so wines with high concentrations will have lower pH readings. As grapes ripen, their acidity reduces to the point where overripe grapes contain almost none at all.

Different types of wine have different pH ranges as follows (O'Donnell, 2022):

Wine Type	**pH Range**
Dessert wines	Below 3.6
Sweet wines	Below 3.4
Red wines	Below 3.4
White wines	Below 3.3

Wine's low pH helps to preserve it and prevents bacteria from colonizing it. Over time, wine becomes less acidic. Acidity changes the character of a wine—when the pH is higher, the wine is rounder and softer.

When making white wines, the results are better when the pH is lower and the acidity is higher. Dessert wines are less acidic because the grapes are usually very ripe and sweet.

Effects of pH on Wine

pH influences not only the fermentation but also the wine's aroma, color, flavor, aging, and stability. It also affects many of the chemical reactions that occur during fermentation. The pH needs to remain stable throughout the winemaking process.

Achieving the right pH has many benefits. It ensures that the color, aroma, and flavors will be stable and fermentation happens smoothly. If acidity is too low, the wine will have poor flavor and body, and may even turn brownish. If you wish to do MLF, most of the bacteria won't survive if the pH is around 3.0 (O'Donnell, 2022).

There are other ways in which pH can affect your wine:

- Oxidation risks are reduced with a low pH (3.0 to 3.4) and increase when the pH is higher (3.6 to 4.0.).
- The wine has a deeper color at a low pH (3.0 to 3.4), but it becomes lighter at a higher pH (3.6 to 4.0). This is the reason why lighter-colored red wines may be described as "wimpy."
- At a low pH (3.0 to 3.4), red wine will be ruby red, but it will develop browner hues at a pH of 3.6 to 4.0 (O'Donnell, 2022).

Altering pH Levels

Wine pH indicates how much acid and potassium are present, as well as the ratio of malic acid to tartaric acid. Ensure that the must and juice are at the right pH before adding yeast to start the fermentation. The pH can be altered in various ways (O'Donnell, 2022):

- MLF produces less acidic wines—this is the preferred option and works well.
- You can blend wines with different acid levels to raise or lower the pH.
- A chemical solution—such as adding tartaric, citric, and malic acids—can be used but most winemakers prefer to avoid this, as these substances are inherently unstable and may compromise wine quality.

Take pH readings before and after attempts to alter the pH level of your must and juice.

PREVENTING OXIDATION

Oxygen and wine are not good bedfellows, although tiny amounts of oxygen help to produce a stable wine with a reasonable shelf life. Red wines benefit from some oxygen to smooth out tannins and stabilize the color, especially during aging. Controlled oxygen exposure during fermentation helps the yeast survive.

When too much oxygen is released into the wine during winemaking, this can be detrimental to the flavor and aromas. There are several ways to prevent this (Goldhawke, 2022):

- In cool, wet seasons, the Botrytis fungus may develop in vineyards. This releases an enzyme called laccase that compromises the wine's flavors and aromas. Once it enters the must, the enzyme cannot be removed, and it even survives in a high sulfur dioxide environment. Prevent Botrytis from spreading through your vineyard by ensuring that the canopy allows good air circulation between the bunches. If your grapes were affected, no oxygen should reach your must, as the enzyme this fungus produces loves oxygen.
- During winemaking, the wine will be moved from tanks and barrels to bottles. All these contain air, and contact with oxygen is inevitable when the wine is being transferred. To reduce oxidation, use an inert gas cover. Place carbon dioxide in the form of dry ice on the surface of the grape must so it forms a protective blanket. You can also use this during racking. Post-fermentation, ensure that you fill the entire barrel or bottle with wine to limit the wine's contact with oxygen.
- Sulfur dioxide or sulfite helps prevent oxidation when added to the wine.
- Wine barrels are porous and soak up some of the wine, which creates an empty space in the barrel. Ethanol and water in the wine can also evaporate. This means that wine barrels may need to be topped up so that there is no oxygen-containing headspace.
- When wine ages in bottles, it may experience oxidation. Choosing the right natural or synthetic cork or screw cap will prevent oxygen from entering the bottle

MANAGING SULFITES

Sulfur dioxide, or sulfite, is an important additive in winemaking. It is a natural byproduct of alcoholic fermentation by yeasts, although the amount naturally found in wines is negligible. Sulfites are augmented to prevent oxidation, preserve the wine, and facilitate proper aging. As a new winemaker, you can go sulfite-free, but this could lead to the proliferation of undesirable compounds. Adding sulfur dioxide slows the natural processes that would ultimately turn the wine into vinegar.

A dash of just 30 to 50 parts per million (ppm) used before fermentation starts is enough to keep undesirable bacteria and yeast strains in check. If the wine undergoes MLF, very little sulfur dioxide needs to be added after fermentation. If you are making crisp white wines without MLF, you will need to add sulfur dioxide immediately after the primary fermentation is finished (Halbach, 2019).

Over time, the sulfur dioxide will react with oxygen and other substances in the wine, which gradually reduces the sulfates present. Racking and bottling each consume around 10 to 12 ppm of sulfur dioxide. You could add 30 to 40 ppm extra during the first aging period, and allow it to drop naturally to what you require for bottling (Haibach, 2019).

Sulfur Dioxide Requirements

After fermentation, you will need to maintain a molecular sulfur dioxide level of 0.8 ppm. The higher the wine's pH, the more sulfur dioxide will be required. Use the table below to guide you.

pH	Free Sulfur Dioxide
2.9	11
3.0	13
3.1	17
3.2	21
3.3	26
3.4	33
3.5	41
3.6	51
3.7	65
3.8	81
3.9	102
4.0	128

Determining How Much Sulfite Is in Your Wine

Total sulfites means all the sulfur dioxide naturally present in the wine, together with that which has been added. Free sulfites refer to the sulfur dioxide that has not reacted with anything else in the wine and is available to prevent microbial growth or attach to oxygen molecules. There are two ways to measure free sulfur dioxide: the ripper method and the aeration-oxidation method. The second is more complicated but very accurate, while the ripper method is quick and easy to do. You can obtain kits from winemaking stores with the necessary equipment and solutions to run these tests. Always wear gloves and goggles when conducting these tests, as you will be working with powerful acids. Keep some baking soda handy to neutralize any spills.

If the free sulfur dioxide is too low, you can adjust this by using potassium metabisulfite. This adds about 57% more free sulfur dioxide. The calculation is as follows (Haibach, 2019):

(ppm of free sulfur dioxide needed) x liters of wine ÷ 0.57 = (milligrams of potassium metabisulfite to add)

Remember to dissolve the metabisulfite completely in a small glass of water or wine before adding it to the wine. Stir it in thoroughly until it is well combined. A small gram scale will help you be more precise.

Making Wines With and Without Sulfites

Sulfur dioxide has relatively recently been determined to be beneficial for creating aromas and textures, giving the wine structure, and for aging. Sulfur modifies tannins and anthocyanins, altering the wine's color and mouthfeel. Aromatic compounds such as esters and thiols are changed by adding sulfites, and different results can be obtained by either adding sulfates or not. The effects are long-lasting and persist, even in the bottle.

One of the newest findings at wineries opting for more natural forms of fermentation is that wines, where no sulfite is added, tend to fight oxygen earlier in the process and become accustomed to it, so they are less likely to oxidize. Winemakers need to be more careful about oxidation when sulfate is added early in the fermentation process. No-sulfur wines taste older when they are young, but their fruity flavors are enhanced as they age. The wine retains its flavor and aromas over time. Tannins are softer and colors lighter.

Adding Oak

Oak chips can be added during secondary fermentation to encourage the formation of tannins and add flavor. They are usually used for red wines, but you can use them when making white wines, too. Oak adds structure, stabilizes the wine's color, and improves its shelf life. When used with light, fruity whites, the oak adds depth and complexity to the flavor.

To use oak chips, simply add them to the wine in the fermentation vessel so the wine absorbs the tannins and flavors directly. Alternatively, soak them in wine or water for a few days before adding them to the fermenter. This means the flavors and tannins will enter the liquid first. If you want a more subtle flavor, you can also brew a tea with the oak chips and add it to the wine.

Use about 56 to 113 grams of chips per 19 liters (2 to 4 ounces of chips per 5 gallons) of wine. Monitor your wine carefully, as the oak can impart flavor very quickly. Start tasting the wine two to three days after adding the oak and continue until the oaky flavor becomes noticeable. When you are happy with the flavor, remove the oak (Kraus, 2022).

Once your wine is fermented, stabilized, clarified, and bottled, you will then begin the aging process, which turns a good wine into a great wine.

5

AGING GRACEFULLY

> *Wine is one of the most civilized things in the world and one of the most natural things in the world that has been brought to greatest perfection, and it offers a greater range for enjoyment and appreciation than possibly any other purely sensory thing.*
>
> — ERNEST HEMMINGWAY

> *Age is just a number. It's totally irrelevant unless, of course, you happen to be a bottle of wine.*
>
> — JOAN COLLINS

In this exciting chapter, you'll discover why aging is important in winemaking and how it enables you as the winemaker to create a refined end product. This chapter will guide you through the process of aging or maturing your wine.

DEGASSING YOUR WINE

Once the fermentation is completed, you will need to stabilize and clarify your wine before you can begin the aging or maturation process. The first step is to degas your wine to remove trapped carbon dioxide so it doesn't start foaming when you open the container. This is not as critical if you intend to age your wine for an extended period of six to ten months, as the carbon dioxide will gradually work its way out of the wine via the airlock (*Degassing Wine*, n.d.).

Degassing can be done by using a long-handled spoon or racking cane to agitate the mix so the carbon dioxide is released. If you have smaller fermentation vessels such as carboys, you can put them on top of your clothes washer during the spin cycle, which works very well. (Make sure that it doesn't vibrate off the washer, however.) You can also use specialized equipment such as wine whips.

STABILIZING YOUR WINE AFTER FERMENTATION

Although wines might appear clear after bottling, they might look a little opaque with sediment at the bottom of the bottles after a few weeks. Stabilizing and clarifying your wines will prevent this. This is particularly important for white and rosé wines.

Procedures

There are several ways in which you can stabilize and clarify your wine (Eisenman, n.d.-b):

Racking

Racking is when the sediment accumulated on the bottom of wine storage containers (lees) is separated from the wine. Place the wine vessel on a table or bench. Set a second, clean container on the floor and siphon the wine out of the first vessel into the new one, leaving the lees behind. White wines are racked three times as follows:

- after fermentation stops to remove the yeast lees
- after the wine has been hot and cold stabilized
- just before bottling

Red wines are only racked after MLF is completed. Dark reds may be racked two or three times during the first year and every six months thereafter.

Fining

Fining is when certain materials are added to the wine to remove haze, bitterness, unwanted colors, and so on. Fining materials include egg white, bentonite clay, casein, gelatin, activated carbon, and Sparkolloid (a mixture of cellulose and diatomaceous earth). These bond with suspended particles, making them larger so they precipitate out of the wine. Unlike filtration, fining may remove tannins, phenols, and proteins. Winemakers take samples and do bench tests to determine which fining material works best and how much to use.

Filtration

Most wineries use both fining and filtration to stabilize and clarify their wines. Filtration removes unwanted particles mechanically without altering any of the wine's fundamental characteristics.

Stabilization Techniques

White and rosé wines are often stored at room temperature but chilled in the refrigerator before serving, so they need to withstand a range of temperatures without changing character. Removing excess protein stabilizes these wines and halts the fermentation. Bentonite is usually used to remove proteins—but you will need to have the wine laboratory tested to determine how much bentonite to add. The process is more effective if the wine is filtered before using bentonite.

The easiest way to stabilize white and rosé wines is to store them at -2 °C (28 °F) for about a week so the excess protein dissipates (Eisenman, n.d.-b). You can do this at higher temperatures, but the process takes longer. To check the wine's stability, place a glass of the wine in the coldest part of your refrigerator for a few days. As the wine returns to room temperature, observe whether any crystals or sediment form. These wines oxidize easily and should be handled carefully during stabilization.

Red wines are also stabilized by chilling. Because they are served at room temperature and the dark color hides any sediment, most home winemakers don't chill them before bottling.

Some winemakers use both methods by first filtering the sediment out of the wine and then chilling it as detailed above so the tartrate dissipates. The cold wine is then either racked or filtered to remove the bentonite and tartrate lees. Combining the two methods is very effective, as the tartrate crystalizes at the top of the wine, and the bentonite lees are less compacted, so they are easier to rack and filter out. Because the two processes are done simultaneously, the vessel need not be opened as often and there is less chance of oxidation.

Stabilizing Sweet Wines

If wine contains more than 0.2% residual sugar, it is considered unstable. Should it continue fermenting in the bottle, it usually cannot be recovered, and the entire batch will be ruined. You can remove excess sugar before bottling by (Eisenman, n.d.-b):

- removing the yeast using a sterile filter
- adding potassium sorbate just before bottling
- killing the yeast by increasing the alcohol content
- pasteurizing the wine, which will also kill the yeast

The alcohol content needs to be at around 18% alcohol per volume to stabilize wines that contain residual sugar, so this method is normally impractical. Pasteurization is rarely used, as it tends to change the character and flavor of the wine.

Chill the wine to at least 7.2 °C (45 °F) and allow the yeast to settle. Rack or filter the wine to remove as much yeast as possible and wait for the wine to return to room temperature. Restart the fermentation and continue fermenting until it stops naturally. You may need to restart the fermentation several times. The yeast will consume the nutrients in the wine until they are exhausted. This technique stabilizes sweet wines very effectively but is usually done by more experienced winemakers (Eisenman, n.d.-b).

Alternatively, proceed as above but don't restart the fermentation after racking or filtering out the yeast. Instead, do a tight filtration, ensuring that the sulfur dioxide content remains at 0.8 ppm and keeping the wine cold. Before bottling, filter the wine using a 0.45 micron filter to remove all remaining yeast and bacteria. For this method to be effective, all your equipment, corks, and bottles must be sterile (Eisenman, n.d.-b)

There is a third way to stabilize sweet wine. Freeze a portion of the wine to be used as a reserve. Then, ferment the wine again until it becomes quite dry and store it as you usually would. Just before you are ready to bottle it, raise the sulfur dioxide levels to 0.8 milligrams per liter of wine and add 250 milligrams potassium sorbate per liter to stop the yeast cells from reproducing. Add enough of the sweet reserve to provide the required amount of sugar. Potassium sorbate is most effective when added to wines with a low yeast content. You can add sugar to the wine but using sweet reserve provides better flavor.

Stabilizing Wines Containing Malic Acid

It is not advisable to bottle red wines when they are high in malic acid, as the wine will develop undesirable traits. The best way to stabilize these wines is to ensure that they have completed MLF before bottling. Encourage MLF by (Eisenman, n.d.-b):

- adding pinches of sulfur dioxide during crushing—around 30 to 40 milligrams per liter
- keeping the wine temperature above 20 °C (68 °F)
- keeping the pH above 3.3. to encourage bacterial activity
- inoculating the wine with a commercial form of malolactic bacteria
- maintaining yeast lees in your wine for several weeks following the completion of the sugar fermentation to encourage MLF

You can also use lysozyme when bottling wines containing malolactic bacteria. This is a naturally occurring enzyme found in human tears that has potent antimicrobial properties. This kills these bacteria, and they degrade into harmless substances.

Lysozyme is best added just before bottling for red wines, as the effect is short-lived.

CLARIFYING RED WINE

Yeast, bacteria, and excessive protein, tartrate, or phenolic polymers cause most of the problems with wine clarity. When red wines are aged in bulk for at least a year before bottling, this resolves most stability and clarity problems. However, white and rosé wines often need special treatment to become clear and stable.

Yeast and bacteria disperse from the wine within a few weeks, although MLF can disturb the mixture. Therefore, it's best to wait until MLF has completed before attempting to filter or clarify the wine.

Protein is naturally present in grapes, and this gets into the wine. The particles are minute, but when the wine becomes warm, the proteins form chains and become visible, often settling at the bottom of the vessel. When the protein dissipates, the wine can become very cloudy and unsightly. Protein hazes are rarely problematic in red wines, as the excess protein precipitates out early in the winemaking process.

Grapes contain potassium and tartaric acid, which combine to form potassium bitartrate (cream of tartar). Only small amounts can dissolve in grape juice, and even less persists once alcohol is formed during fermentation. Cold wines hold less tartrate than warm wines. After fermentation, potassium bitartrate is present in significant quantities in the wine, and tartrate crystals form as it dissipates. These wines need to be stabilized at cold temperatures to remove the excess tartrate before bottling.

Phenolic compounds give wine many of its characteristics—flavor, color, bitterness, and astringency. These compounds increase gradually and can make red wines cloudy with unusual amounts of sediment. Fining with protein-based materials such as gelatin, casein, egg white, or isinglass usually removes phenolic compounds. This is done a few weeks before bottling. All red wines will develop some bottle deposits after a few years.

AGING YOUR WINE: OVERVIEW

Wine can be aged in several ways before bottling—and it will age in the bottles, too. Winemakers often don't release all their stock immediately, and consumers can also keep the wine for a while before drinking it.

Aging wine successfully means controlling the amount of oxygen that is present. As mentioned previously, aging the wine too quickly usually gives it a brownish hue. If there is not much oxygen available, the aromatics will develop slowly. In red wines, color pigments bind with tannins to form heavier compounds that precipitate out. This turns the wine orange-red and sediment settles on the bottom of the bottles.

The ideal temperature for wine storage is around 12 °C (55 °F). If temperatures are warmer, the wine loses some of its finer points. Too low a temperature can slow the chemical reactions and the bottles might also break if they freeze (Martellotto, 2022).

The following factors enable wine to age well (Martellotto, 2022):

- Sugars protect the wine against oxidation, as these oxidize before tannins or aromatic compounds. Dessert wines can be aged for very long periods.
- Tannins precipitate out of red wines as they age, which reduces the oxidation of aromatic compounds.
- Wines with a high alcohol content age well and can be kept for longer than most wines.
- Acid is a natural preservative that increases the shelf life of wine. Acidity declines with age. If the wine is low in acid to begin with, it will become imbalanced as it ages.

How the wine ultimately tastes depends on the winemaker's choices during aging. For example, there might be extended contact with the grape skins, enabling more tannins, colors, and aromatic compounds to be extracted. The winemaker might decide to allow the wine to stay in contact with the lees for slightly longer to create a creamy texture and flavor.

STAVE TO BARREL: CHOOSING THE RIGHT VESSEL

Aging generally improves the quality of the wine, although it will decline if it is stored for too long. Different storage containers are used during aging. In this section, you will find out more about the effects different storage containers have on your wine.

General Considerations

Besides the characteristics and flavors you might want the wine to develop in storage, it's important to consider how much wine you will be making. Carboys will be great for storing small volumes, but if your production runs to a few hundred liters, then this will be very impractical.

Regardless of the material they are made of, most wine vats have a cylindrical shape, although cubic, pyramidal, ovoid, or rectangular ones are also used. Each shape confers different advantages. For example, ovoid vats allow the wine to circulate continuously, so the lees are held in suspension without the need for stirring. This creates fuller, more concentrated wines.

Glass Carboys

Glass carboys make great storage containers for smaller wine volumes but allow light in. You can cover them or paint over the outside, although this means you won't be able to see what's happening inside. Unfortunately, carboys are fragile, and you will need to handle them carefully so they don't crack or fall and break.

Wooden Barrels

Wooden barrels are the iconic form of wine storage. Originally used in France and Italy, the use of oak barrels eventually spread worldwide. The volume of the barrels varies depending on your region, and each size goes by a different, usually French, name. In Bordeaux, a *barrique* holds 225 liters (59.4 gallons) of wine, equivalent to 300 standard bottles. The next size up is a *tonneau,* which holds 900 liters (237.7 gallons). In Burgundy, a standard wine barrel holds 228 liters (60 gallons), equivalent to 304 standard bottles of wine, and is called a *pièce*. Age your wine in barrels if you want the wood, together with tiny amounts of oxygen, to alter the wine's flavor profile and tannins (*The Role of Barrels,* 2016).

Oak is used for barrels because of the flavors it imparts. New oak barrels in particular confer their aromatic compounds and tannins to the wine stored inside. Once a barrel has been used multiple times, however, the flavor and tannins it adds to the wine will reduce. European and American oak confers slightly different flavor profiles: European oak creates vanilla and caramel notes, while American oak creates a coconut flavor and, occasionally, dill.

The toasting of the barrel also confers different flavors that vary from barrel to barrel. Below is an overview of how toasting may affect wine tastes and flavors (*Oak Barrels and Containers,* 2021):

- Light-brown toasts that barely skim the wood surface will deliver fruity, vanilla notes, together with the flavor of new wood.
- Medium toasts—up to 5 millimeters (0.1 inch) thick—are popular, especially for full-bodied wines, and result in wines with more tannins and complex flavors. Flavors are reminiscent of smokey cocoa, vanilla, coffee, dried fruit, and honey.

- Robust toasting—over 7 millimeters (0.2 inch) thick—raises the smoky flavor of the wine, delivering toasted caramel, tobacco, and charcoal flavors, together with many others.

Oak barrels allow minuscule amounts of oxygen to reach the wine, enabling winemakers to further control wine flavors.

Barrels from France, Slovenia, and North America are imported globally because of the flavors they produce. Chestnut wood is also used on a limited basis, although it allows more oxygen into the wine than oak. In the United States, producers once used redwoods for storage and transport, but this is now a rare occurrence.

Benefits of Barrel Storage

Storage in oak barrels is especially beneficial for red table wines, as this reduces astringency, improves color, and creates more complex flavors. This works especially well when the wine is aged in one 982-liter (500-gallon) barrel for at least two to three years, often followed by bottle aging, which happens at a slower rate—anything from two to twenty years (Amerine, 2023). Dessert wines such as sweet cherries also benefit from cask aging, although they should not be left in the barrel too long. Rosé and dry red wines should only be aged briefly before being clarified and bottled.

Nearly all table wines are sold and consumed before they are two years old (Amerine, 2023). While dry white wines may have better clarity if they are aged for short periods, this is rarely necessary these days because better clarification methods now exist. Earlier bottling reduces costs and produces fresher flavors with more fruitiness.

Clay Vessels (Amphorae)

Clay vessels have been preferred traditionally for both fermentation and storage. Their use in winemaking is making a tremendous comeback. They can be used for virtually any grape variety, and top wine producers are investing in their collections. Clay is a neutral material that won't change wine flavors. These vessels are slightly porous, allowing tiny amounts of oxygen to enter brews. Some producers age all their wines in amphorae and then mix them with other wines to diversify their flavor profiles.

Stainless Steel Tanks

As mentioned previously, using stainless steel equipment has many advantages for winemakers. Wine can also be aged in stainless steel tanks. This provides an oxygen-free environment and won't add any additional flavors to the wine. Instead, the aromas created during primary and secondary fermentation will be more concentrated. Storing wine in stainless steel won't change its essential character.

Advantages and Disadvantages of Stainless Steel Storage Tanks

Advantages	Disadvantages
Durable	High initial costs
Easy to clean and sterilize	Lack of oxygen creates wines with muted flavors
Available in different sizes	Additional racking is required to deliver oxygen to the wine
Creates an oxygen-free, dark environment	
Won't add additional flavors and concentrates existing ones	
Are good heat conductors	

Bottles

Before bottling, wines are often blended and filtered. Some commercial winemakers also add antiseptics to prevent spoilage. When the same wine is stored in several different barrels, each acquires different characteristics depending on the qualities of the particular barrel. This means the batch might need to be blended to create a uniform color and flavor profile. If a wine has an undesirable color or too much acidity, it can be blended with another to correct these defects. Blending often adds complexity to the wine, improving its quality.

While wine can be aged in the bottle, this is not always a good idea, especially when you consider that around 90% of wines that are commercially produced are meant to be consumed either straight away or within five years of bottling. There are a few traits that make wines more suitable for bottle aging (Weatherwax, n.d.):

- Wines high in sugar, such as ports and dessert wines, are more suitable for aging, and some can be aged for as long as 100 years.
- If a wine is not fortified—in other words, if a distilled spirit is not added to it—then it is more likely to turn vinegary over time because the alcohol levels are unstable. Non-fortified wines with lower alcohol levels are more suited to aging.
- The more acidic a non-fortified wine is, the better it will age in a wine cellar.
- Wines high in tannins are ideal for bottle aging, as they will mellow with age.

Plastic Containers

Plastic containers or barrels are an option for small producers and hobby winemakers, but these are usually avoided by larger wineries. There are also environmental issues associated with plastic production and waste. Using plastic for storing wine is entirely up to you. On the plus side, colored plastic lets in little light or oxygen. Tanks and containers can be filled with oak chips to even out the tannins and improve the wine's flavor. You will need to rack the wine regularly so it doesn't lose its flavors and to deliver oxygen to the wine.

Now that you know more about wine aging and storage, it's time to find out more about the art of blending. This is an age-old skill that will enable you to get the most out of your wine before bottling.

6

THE ART OF BLENDING

> *Wine that gladdens human hearts.*
>
> — PSALM 104:15, THE BIBLE

> *Originality is a little more than the fine blending of influences.*
>
> — TEJU COLE

The true craft of winemaking comes to the fore when wines are blended to achieve the complex, balanced flavors that are the hallmarks of a unique, memorable wine. In this chapter, you'll discover how to develop this special skill.

WHAT IS BLENDING?

Wine drinkers generally know very little about the mysterious art of blending, even though nearly all wines are blends, be they different grape varieties, vineyards, or barrels. In brief, blending is when different batches of wine are combined, resulting in a wine that is balanced, consistent, and complex with many aromas, tastes, and textures. Blending means you can, for instance, add interest to a young wine. When making your own wines, you will see that each batch has different characteristics, aromas, textures, and flavors. This can be a good thing, as it gives you plenty of options for developing your own special blends. Blends are often created in tiny increments, so the process is very time-consuming.

Some wineries employ special teams to create their blends. After the individual wines have been tasted, blending starts. Everyone's samples are blind-tested by the others until a final blend is selected.

Winemakers begin with a base blend, which forms the foundation. If the wine is going to be Cabernet-based, for example, Cabernet should account for 60% to 65% of the final blend (Sullivan, 2023). Although other wine varieties will be added, the blenders need to ensure that Cabernet characteristics predominate. Blending may take anything from a few hours to several months.

Most winemakers create and evaluate numerous blends before making a final decision. They begin by blending larger percentages and then fine-tuning, adding just 1 to 2% of a particular wine. Even these tiny ratios can make a surprisingly big difference to the final blend (Sullivan, 2023).

Once you have decided on a blend, you then need to scale it up, keeping to the same ratios. Results might be unexpected: two tannin-rich wines could create a smoother blend, while two smooth wines could create a tart, unpleasant one. It's best to not have any preconceived ideas but to continue experimenting until you find the sweet spot.

Another important consideration for blending wines is the timing. Avoid blending wines too soon after harvest, as the flavors are still developing or are still undergoing MLF. Early vintages will be ready to taste before late harvests, for example.

WINE CHARACTERISTICS

There are several terms winemakers use to describe a wine's taste. These are grouped into four categories, as follows (Fragiacomo, n.d.):

- the body of the wine
- whether it's sweet or dry
- acidity levels
- fruity or other flavors

These describe the wine's overall characteristics and help consumers identify the types of wine they enjoy drinking. Let's unpack this some more.

Acidity

Wines produced in cool climates are more acidic than those produced in warmer regions. Daytime temperature variations increase acidity. This is why grapes are often grown in mountainous areas, where there is a marked difference between daytime and nighttime temperatures. For example, wine grown in the Rocky Mountains has particularly high acidity due to the very high daytime temperature variation and relatively cold average temperatures.

Besides preserving the wine, acidity is crucial for determining a wine's structure, freshness, and crispness. Acidic wines leave a tart, tangy sensation on your palate that is caused by organic acids in the wine. Low-acid wines may taste flat, dull, sharp, and sour. Acidity balances out sweetness, tannins, and body. More acidic wines may be described as bright, refreshing, and vibrant when compared to less acidic wines.

Tannins

Tannins occur naturally in grape skins, seeds, and stems. They are more prevalent in red wines, which are fermented with these components present. Tannins impart a drying, astringent sensation to your palate. Wines high in tannin tend to be full-bodied and robust, while low-tannin wines tend to be softer and gentler.

Sweetness

Wines can be either very dry or exceptionally sweet, depending on the grape variety used and the winemaker's choices. Sweetness is determined by residual sugars that remain behind after fermentation is completed. Surprisingly, this doesn't always result in a sweeter wine, especially if it is high in tannins or acidity. The opposite also applies, as exceptionally fruity wines can be sweet-tasting. Sweetness may balance more astringent aspects of the wine, including acidity, tannins, and body. Dryness or sweetness is ultimately determined by how the wine tastes. Sweetness can be enhanced by fruitiness or any sweet-tasting spices it contains. Tannins and high acidity tend to make wines drier. Sweet varietals include Asti Spumante, Cienna, Moscato, Muscat, and White Zinfandel.

Body

"Body" is a term used to describe the texture, weight, and mouthfeel of the wine. Alcohol levels, acidity, and tannins all influence this aspect. The body of a wine is enhanced by the amount of tannins and alcohol present, together with sweetness. Light-bodied wines are usually more delicate, with lower alcohol and tannins. Full-bodied wines are frequently bold with a strong texture and are characterized by high alcohol levels and tannins. Medium-bodied wines fall somewhere in between. Full-bodied varietals include Chardonnay, Durif, Pinotage, Sauternes, and Shiraz.

Alcohol

As you might have guessed, alcohol is a key element of a wine's flavor profile and body, and this is what keeps it in balance. A wine's alcohol content depends on elements such as the grape variety, the local climate, and the winemaking techniques used. Higher-alcohol wines are inclined to be full-bodied with a decisive mouthfeel and are warmer on the palate. Lower-alcohol wines are lighter and more refreshing. The alcohol should balance out the other elements such as sweetness, tannins, and acidity.

WINE FLAVOR PROFILES

Several things determine the flavor profile of a wine, including (Serpo, 2023):

- grape varieties used
- climate and terroir
- winemaking techniques and aging

Wine Flavor Categories

Wine flavors are often described in terms of fruits other than grapes, which can be confusing. During fermentation, the grapes release many of the same chemicals that are found in other fruits. Oak aging is often responsible for most of the secondary and tertiary flavors described by sommeliers and winemakers. These may include sweet or dry spices and even buttery or creamy notes.

Fruit Flavors

These flavors may be described as anything from bright and fresh to dark and jammy, depending on the wine style and grape varieties. Below are some examples (Serpo, 2023):

- White wines: Apple, apricot, melon, peach, pear, and pineapple
- Red wines: Blackberry, blackcurrant, cherry, fig, plum, and raspberry
- Rosé wines: Cranberry, red currant, strawberry, and watermelon
- Sparkling wines: Citrus, green apple, red berries, and tropical fruits

Floral Flavors

These are delicate and often aromatic. Normally a feature of white and rosé wines, they are occasionally present in red wines. These include (Serpo, 2023):

- White wines: Elderflower, honeysuckle, jasmine, and orange blossom
- Red wines: Peony, rose, and violet
- Rosé wines: Lavender, hibiscus, and rose
- Sparkling wines: Acacia, iris, and lily

Herb and Spice Flavors

These are imbued by the grape variety, terroir, and the winemaking process. They include (Serpo, 2023):

- White wines: Basil, ginger, lemongrass, nutmeg, and white pepper
- Red wines: Black pepper, cinnamon, clove, eucalyptus, and mint
- Rosé wines: Pink peppercorn, rosemary, and thyme
- Sparkling wines: Allspice, anise, and fennel

Earthy and Mineral Flavors

Linked to the terroir, these add depth and complexity to the flavor profile. They include (Serpo, 2023):

- White wines: Chalk, flint, oyster shell, sea salt, and wet stone
- Red wines: Graphite, mushroom, slate, truffle, and wet leaves
- Rosé wines: Clay and limestone

- Sparkling wines: Crushed rock, mineral water, and salinity

Oak and Wood Flavors

These are created during the aging process, especially if the wine was stored in oak barrels. Examples include (Serpo, 2023):

- White wines: Butterscotch, caramel, dill, and toasted almond
- Red wines: Cedar, mocha, smoke, toasted oak, and vanilla
- Rosé wines: Charred wood and sandalwood
- Sparkling wines: Brioche, hazelnut, marzipan, and toasted bread

Secondary and Tertiary Flavors

Secondary flavors are created during fermentation, while tertiary flavors are produced when the wine ages in the bottle. These include (Serpo, 2023):

- White wines: Almond, baked apple, beeswax, honey, and petrol
- Red wines: Dried fruit, game, leather, soy sauce, and tobacco
- Rosé wines: Dried herbs and potpourri
- Sparkling wines: Bread dough, butter, cream, and yeast

BLENDING WINE AT HOME

Blending wine sounds simple—but don't be fooled. Part science and part art, it's a little more complex than it appears. Commercial wineries blend wines to ensure consistency of their varietals from one year to the next. This reduces any annual variations that might creep in. Another reason for blending, which applies to home winemakers, too, is to improve the wine. Blending combines two or three wines, thereby creating something better than the individual wines by themselves. To blend wine successfully, you won't only need to know the process but also require a good palate and the ability to envision the different flavors you will create. Blending is an art—it takes time and experience to develop this winemaking skill.

The Mechanics of Wine Blending—Pearson's Square

Pearson's Square is a handy tool you can use to determine the right proportions when blending to ensure that your final result is properly balanced. You can use this technique to blend the following (*Blending Wine With Pearson's Square*, 2014):

- low-alcohol wines with high-alcohol ones to even out the alcohol levels
- wines with different acidity levels to produce a more balanced wine
- wine and brandy when fortifying a wine

You can also use Pearson's Square to calculate how much additional sugar you need to add to raise the alcohol content of a completed wine.

Taking measurements means you have some control over the outcome, rather than mixing wines at random. For instance, if you know the alcohol content of two wines you wish to blend together to even out the alcohol level, you can predict the outcome to some extent. Using Pearson's Square won't enable you to determine how the wine tastes—for that, you'll need to actually taste it—but you can control the measurable aspects of the wine when you are blending.

Example

You want to blend two wines to reduce the level of acidity in one of them, which is particularly acidic. One has a titrate acid level of 1.10%, whereas the other has an acid level of 55%. You decide that you want to create a wine with an acidity level of 70%. Your Pearson's Square will look like this:

____

||

[55 40]

||

||

||

[70]

||

||

||

[110 15]

|_________]

The numbers at the top right and bottom left of the square represent the acidity of the wines to be blended. In the center is the number of the acidity level you want to achieve. The numbers on the right of 55 and 110 are the ones that you calculate. The difference between 70 and 55 is 15, and the difference between 110 and 70 is 40. This provides the ratio needed to create the desired result. In this example, you need to blend 15 parts of the 1.10% wine with 40 parts of the 55% wine to obtain a wine with 70% acidity (*Blending to Improve Homemade Wines*, n.d.).

Guidelines for Blending Wines at Home

Here are a few hints and tips for blending your own homemade wines:

- Avoid blending wines that are hopelessly flawed. You can, however, blend quality wines that have a single correctable defect. Blending won't turn a poor wine into a high-quality one.

- Blending works better when done soon after fermentation. This protects the end result from oxidation and means the two wines will age together as a unit rather than separately.
- Having said that, you might need to wait before blending young red wines in particular because their flavors won't be fully developed. This means you won't be able to get an accurate idea of the final flavor of the blend.
- Decide what you want to achieve with your blending. Be specific. Blend to adjust a wine feature such as color or acidity, to alter the flavor notes of a wine, or to simulate a commercial wine you enjoy.
- Do test blends with small amounts before blending large quantities. Get a few friends to help. Ask someone to mix the blend, and allow the others to do a blind tasting. Once you are happy with the combination, you can add a third wine to the blend. To avoid becoming hopelessly muddled and inebriated, have a bucket handy so you can spit out the wine.
- In between each tasting, you and your fellow tasters will need to cleanse your palate to enable you to taste the next blend accurately. You can eat something bland, such as crackers or pineapple, and even sniff coffee beans.
- Take notes.
- Wait at least a day after you've decided on a good combination. Retaste your blend when your palate is fresh and you are more clear-headed. Avoid overthinking. Take a sip or two and think about the wine from a drinker's perspective.
- It's best to filter your wines after blending. When you blend, some fines might precipitate out of the wine. Wait a few days after blending so this process can be completed. This is unpredictable but be prepared in case it happens.

- Blending wines from the same year usually ensures better results. There is also less chance of fines precipitating out of the wine. When older wines are blended with younger ones, they tend to become sharp and harsh.
- Blend wines with the same character. Heavy reds should be combined with heavy reds, for example, Cabernet with Merlot. Blending a Merlot with a Riesling won't create good results (*Blending to Improve Homemade Wines*, n.d.).

TASTING AND ADJUSTING

Taking measurements and following guidelines is all very well, but the taste and flavor of the wine are the real issues. To become proficient at blending, you need to be able to identify the wine's good points, establishing what makes it special. The weaknesses of a wine are usually easier to identify—an unpleasant aftertaste, a bland flavor, or something more measurable such as color or acidity. You can only start considering what wine will complement another when you know exactly how the wine works on your palate. The two wines should balance one another, compensating for one another's weak points, while adding to both their strengths. The art comes from knowing which wines will fuse together harmoniously.

ACHIEVING BALANCE AND COMPLEXITY

If a wine has fewer than three characteristics and flavors, wine drinkers will generally consider it to be uninteresting. This is often the case with cheaper bulk wines. Complex wines contain several different flavors and have a well-defined character. There are dozens of individual notes to tickle your taste buds. Winemakers achieve complexity by following good grape cultivation practices, doing careful fermentations, and blending their wines.

Better-quality wines are more complex, so consumers pay premium prices for them. Blending grape varieties to deliver a finished wine has been a common practice for centuries. Examples include Bordeaux wines created by blending Cabernet Sauvignon, Merlot, and Cabernet Franc, as well as champagne made by blending Chardonnay, Pinot Noir, and Pinot Meunier. Thirteen grape varieties are used to create Châteauneuf-du-Pape from France's Rhône Valley (Kuhlken, 2018).

Commercial wineries select grapes for the unique elements they will create and the way they will work together in the finished wine. This is called blending up and means that the different elements of winemaking combine to create a great-tasting wine or vintage.

Some single varieties are delicious on their own, while others work better in blends. As a winemaker, you will learn to appreciate the intricacies of a carefully blended wine and the excitement and freedom of experimenting with different varieties you have made.

HOW TO CREATE THE BEST RED WINE BLEND

Below is a quick tutorial on how to create a blend (Shallenberger, 2016):

1. Choose three or four of your red wines that you believe would be suitable for blending and work well together.
2. Ensure that you have several wine glasses on hand for tasting.

3. Choose one wine that will be the foundation and ensure that about half of your blend consists of that wine.
4. Slowly add the other two or three wines in different amounts, taking careful notes of the results, noting the body, texture, color, and flavor of each blend.
5. When you have arrived at two or three blends that you feel are sufficiently complex and reflect the unique character and flavors of the individual wines, invite a few friends over and get them to do a blind tasting to see which one they prefer.

FAMOUS WINE BLENDS

Red Wines

Red wine blends are created using specific red grape varieties that are usually crushed and fermented separately before combining. Older blends like Bordeaux and Chianti are made using techniques handed down for centuries. Although wine ages and flavors vary, most red blends have red or black fruit undertones.

If you've ever wondered how some European wineries achieve their remarkable blends, read on for some inside information (Rawat, 2022):

- Red Bordeaux is a historic French blend created by blending Merlot, Cabernet Sauvignon, and Cabernet Franc, together with some Petit Verdot, Malbec, or Carménère. This wine exhibits flavor notes like black cherry, chocolate, licorice, and plum.
- Italy's Super Tuscan wine blends are produced using a variety of grapes, including Sangiovese, Merlot, and Cabernet Sauvignon.

- Another Tuscan favorite is Chianti, which is usually 75% Sangiovese grapes, to which Camiolo, Cabernet Sauvignon, or Cabernet Franc are added. It confers savory flavors and complements most Italian dishes and foods.
- Rioja is a well-known Spanish blend, which includes 70% Tempranillo grapes, combined with Graciano, Maturana Tinta, and Mazuelo. Other grapes may also be used to create these blends. Flavor notes include cherry, dill, leather, plum, and vanilla. This was one of the first wines used to make Sangria.

White Wines

White wines have been produced for over 2,500 years, and blending was often standard due to the practice of combining European vineyards. White Bordeaux was first made in the 18th or 19th century, using grapes such as Sauvignon Blanc, Muscadelle, and Sémillon (Rawat, 2022). Unfortunately, many white table wines today are considered to be inferior. Despite this, talented winemakers have continued producing quality white wine blends, which have gained wider appeal in recent years.

White wine blends are made by crushing and fermenting different grape varieties separately before combining them, while traditional methods are used for White Bordeaux, Sauternes, or White Rioja. White wine blends age well in the bottle and often yield citrus and white grape flavors.

Quality white wine blends include (Ravat, 2022):

- The historic White Bordeaux referred to above is synonymous with exquisite quality and age potential. When young, this blend exhibits peach and sweet apple flavors, which turn to candied fruit, custard, and honey as the wine ages, becoming richer in flavor and texture.

- Sauternes is a White Bordeaux wine produced from grapes damaged by noble rot. This confers a sweet, full-bodied flavor to this costly wine.
- White Rioja is a well-known Spanish wine made by blending a variety of grapes, including Garnacha Blanca, Malvasia, Verdejo, and Viura. Flavors include citrus and dried fruit notes. Adding oak to the blend enhances these flavors.
- Southern Rhône White Blend contains a mixture of Grenache Blanc, Roussanne, or Viognier grapes, combined with a smaller amount of Bourboulenc, Clairette, Marsanne, Picpoul, and Ugni Blanc. Although conceived in France's Rhône Valley, it is produced worldwide. Flavors include citrus, spicy notes, and stone fruit.

Once you have mastered the art of blending your homemade wines, the next step is to present them in such a way as to capture attention. They should impress potential consumers at first sight. In the following chapter, you will learn how to achieve this.

A COMMUNITY OF NEW WINEMAKERS

"Wine is the answer. I just don't remember the question."

— ANONYMOUS

How many times had you toyed with the idea of making your own wine before you finally started looking into it seriously? For many people, the interest is there long before they find the confidence to give it a go, and for many others, it stays in their head as a vague idea, never to be truly explored.

Why? People assume winemaking is difficult and time-consuming. They worry they're going to make mistakes, resulting in expensive losses and a lot of frustration. Maybe you were worried about those things, too ... and now you're beginning to see differently.

Winemaking is such a rewarding hobby that I was determined to make it accessible to more people, and that's what led to this book. Now that we're halfway through our journey together, I'd like to ask you to help me reach more of those people who would love to make their own wine but don't quite know how to get started, and to do that, all you need to do is leave a short review.

By leaving a review of this book on Amazon, you'll help new readers find everything they need to unlock the door to a wonderful future of winemaking.

People are looking for this information, just as you were, and your review will make it easier for them to find it and reassure them that winemaking isn't too ambitious a hobby to take up.

Thank you so much for your support. There's a real community spirit amongst winemakers, and that reaches a new level when we're able to connect online, too.

Scan the QR code below for a quick review!

7

BOTTLING AND STORAGE

> *Wine is bottled poetry.*
>
> — ROBERT LOUIS STEVENSON

> *Everyone serves a good wine first and, when people have drunk freely, then the poor wine. But you have kept the good wine until now.*
>
> — JOHN 2:10, THE BIBLE

Once you've made and blended your wine, it's important to consider how you will present it. This is the final phase of winemaking. In this chapter, you'll find everything you need to know about choosing the perfect corks and bottles, creating compelling labels, and storing your wine. These aspects will enhance the wine's appearance and taste.

CHOOSING THE RIGHT BOTTLES AND CORKS

Until around the 17th century, wine was stored in oak barrels and decanted directly from them for drinking. Animal skins were also used for wine storage. Unfortunately, oxygen could get into the wine through these vessels, negatively affecting its quality. Although made for centuries, glass wasn't thick enough to be used for wine storage, but the invention of the coal furnace in the 1600s changed that (Svilane, 2023). The production of heavier, thicker glass wine bottles enabled wine to be transported worldwide. Glass and wine are often synonymous. Glass is also environmentally friendly, as it is fully recyclable and uses fewer natural resources than other packaging.

For winemakers, storing wine in glass has several benefits (Svilane, 2023):

- Glass can be molded into different bottle shapes.
- Modern wine bottles are more robust and less likely to break. Technological improvements over the last 15 years have created lighter bottles.
- Wine can be hermetically sealed in glass to keep oxygen out indefinitely, so wines can be aged for years.
- Glass is inert and doesn't react chemically with the wine. Wine stored in bottles retains its characteristics, flavors, and aromas.
- Wine has an elegant, sophisticated feel when stored in glass. Bag-in-box and paper wine bottles don't provide the same experience. Their production also uses more materials and resources than glass bottles.

Glass Colors

Wines from Champagne, France, are usually stored in green bottles, as are white wines from Mosel in Germany. Wines from Rheingau are bottled in amber glass. The bottles for French Bordeaux wines are usually made from antique (amber-green) glass, while dead leaf green is used for French Burgundian Chardonnay or Pinot Noir.

Wines are bottled in colored glass to maintain their integrity. Although a clear bottle might show off the wine's color, a darker one will protect it from the sun's harmful UV rays. Wine is sensitive to both natural and artificial light. Even an hour of sunlight can produce off-flavors known as "lightstruck" flavors, such as cooked cabbage, rotting leaves, skunk, onion, wet wool, and others.

Consumers expect to see the natural colors of wines such as rosé, Pinot Grigio, and Sauvignon Blanc, so winemakers use clear or flint glass for them. Unfortunately, this increases the wine's susceptibility to UV light. Boxes and cellophane wraps may protect wines bottled in clear glass. Clear and flint glass are reserved for wines that require little or no aging.

Dark green and amber glass provides the best UV protection. Antique green is favored by U.S. winemakers as it delivers UV protection, reduces color fading, and mitigates oxidation. Although tannins protect red wine, darker glass is advisable during aging. Light yellow—dead leaf green—glass is often used for white wines and provides some UV protection.

Wine Bottle Shapes

The grapes used to make the wine determine the bottle's shape. Chardonnays and Pinot Noirs are poured into Burgundy-shaped bottles, reflecting the region in France where these grapes were first grown. The same holds for Cabernet Sauvignon, Merlot, Malbec, and Cabernet Franc, which are bottled in Bordeaux bottles.

There are five basic wine bottle shapes (Tanner, n.d.):

1. Bordeaux bottles, which evolved in Bordeaux, France, are the most popular and are used globally by wine producers. They are tall bottles with short, straight necks, sharply cut shoulders, and straight sides. Associated grapes include Cabernet Franc, Cabernet Sauvignon, Chenin Blanc, Malbec, Merlot, and Sémillon.
2. The Burgundy bottle has a wide base that curves upward to a shorter neck. It has no straight edges and slopes easily from bottom to top. Associated grapes include Chardonnay and Pinot Noir.
3. Rhône bottles are taller, long-necked versions of the Bordeaux bottle. Embossed badges or shields are characteristic of wines grown, made, and bottled in France's Rhône Valley. Associated grapes include Grenache, Marsanne, Mourvèdre, Roussanne, Syrah, and Viognier.
4. The Champagne bottle needs little introduction. It is similar to the Burgundy bottle but is made of much thicker glass to contain the bubbles. It has a large punt—the indent at the bottom. Sparkling wine producers worldwide use this bottle design.

5. Alsace or Rhine bottles are tall, slender, and elegant with a shallow punt at the bottom. They originated on the French-German border and make attractive displays. Associated grapes include Gewürztraminer, Grüner Veltliner, Pino Gris, and Riesling.

The shape of the bottle affects how the wine pours. Bottles with high shoulders and wider openings pour faster and more easily than ones with sloping shoulders and narrower openings. Heavier bottles are easier to handle and pour and indicate good quality. Punts at the base prevent sediment from getting into the wine during pouring. This is particularly important for wines needing decanting. Decanted wines are normally consumed shortly afterward, when the flavors and aromas are at their best.

Choosing Bottles for Homemade Wine

The wine industry standard is a 750-milliliter glass bottle such as green Bordeaux. Another option is the smaller 375-milliliter glass bottle for people who drink wine slowly (David A., 2016). This is a perfect size for gifts and ideal for dessert and ice wines that won't be consumed very quickly. Smaller bottles are used for wines that will be consumed relatively soon after production. These wines are lighter, less complex, and don't need a long time to mature.

Glass gallon jugs are perfect if you want to have a party and serve your own wines. These are usually available in 4-liter (1-gallon) or 2-liter (½-gallon) sizes.

For winemakers who want to store larger wine quantities, a convenient, pre-sanitized 7-liter bag might be the answer. The bag fits into a dispensing box that can be kept on your kitchen counter or in the fridge. The bag collapses as the wine is consumed, so the remainder won't be oxidized. The wine can be stored for up to six months, and it's easier than bottling and corking. Smaller bags are also available (David A., 2016).

Larger bottles of up to 10 liters may be used for wines that will be aged over several years (David A., 2023). These wines are complex and full-bodied, requiring several years to mature. The ratio of air relative to the wine decreases with bottle size, so the wine ages more slowly in a large bottle. This helps prevent oxidation.

Natural Corks Versus Synthetic Closures

A wine bottle closure affects how much oxygen seeps into the wine each year, ultimately affecting its color, flavor, and quality. Glass seals out oxygen but a cork lets in minute quantities. Over time, this can break down the sulfites winemakers add to prevent oxidation and preserve the wine.

There are several different corks to choose from (*Choosing a Wine Cork*, n.d.; Waterhouse, 2015):

- About 250 years ago, natural cork replaced the oiled rags and wooden plugs that previously sealed bottles. For the first time, wines could be aged in bottles—this was the only option for quality wines until about 20 years ago. Cork is derived from the bark of the cork oak tree and is cut from the outside toward the inside. It is harvested every seven years. Most natural cork comes from forests in Portugal and Spain, while Morocco, Algeria, Tunisia, Italy, and France produce smaller amounts. About 1% of natural corks react chemically with the wine in the bottle to create a moldy-smelling substance.
- Agglomerated corks consist of compressed cork granules held together with synthetic binding agents. They are cheaper but less durable than natural corks. Their seal is

intended for wines that will be stored for a short while before consumption. They may disintegrate into the bottle over time.

- Natural disk top (NDT) cork is a combination of natural cork, cork granules, and synthetic binding agents. These corks are agglomerated corks with two disks of natural cork attached to either end. The seal is better than natural and agglomerated cork, and they have some elasticity. They are suitable for medium to long-term storage. However, the glue binding the disks to the rest of the cork can sometimes fail.
- Synthetic corks are made from polyethylene plastic and perform just as well as their natural counterparts. They let in controlled amounts of oxygen but never react with the wine or become tainted. Some sources indicate that synthetic corks let minimal oxygen into the wine and are best for wines that will age over long periods.
- Colmated corks are 90% natural cork combined with a mixture of natural cork granules and glue. These strong, high-quality corks provide good seals and won't disintegrate over time. The natural glue filters into the pores of the cork to strengthen it. This cork provides an excellent seal and won't allow much oxygen into the bottle.
- Screwcaps have two parts: a metal cap with an inside liner that determines how much oxygen the wine receives. This has created a niche market for the manufacturers of screwcap liners, who are rushing to create ones attuned to winemakers' needs. Screwcaps are very consistent.

Synthetic closures perform well, and wine drinkers can choose whether they want the convenience of a screwcap or the ceremony of uncorking a wine. For aging purposes, it's recommended that you consider using natural cork, as this is a tried and tested option.

This could change once synthetic corks and screwcaps have been around long enough to create a decent track record.

The bottle openings for all wine bottles are 19 millimeters (¾ inch) in diameter. Natural cork is sold in four different sizes, from #7 to #10. You can press a #7 cork into the bottle by hand, but you will need a corker for the others. If you want the wine to age quickly, then a #7 cork will be sufficient, but if you want your wines to age for an extended period, then it would be better to use one of the larger sizes. Most winemakers use sizes #8 or #9 to balance aging with good shelf-life. Most commercial wineries use #9 corks, so you'll be in good company if you choose those (Kraus, 2022-c).

WINE LABELS

Most winemakers label their wines, even in a very rudimentary way, to keep track of their inventories. Wine labels should include:

- grapes used
- type of wine
- bottling date
- region
- alcohol content
- amount of sulfides present

If you really want to, you can create personalized wine labels to give your wine bottles a finished, polished look. If you're creative, this is where you can have some fun.

Start by deciding on your colors. Should you use bold accent colors or pale pastels? Think about the colors and flavors of your wine and find a color to represent them. Red wines in dark green bottles often bear labels with darker color schemes or white labels bearing rich red and gold lettering or black text and images. White wine labels are paler, in keeping with the wine's crisp flavors, while rosé wines normally have pink and gold labels. You don't need to follow these trends with your labels, though—many cellars are breaking with tradition to create unusual labels.

A picture tells a thousand words, as the saying goes, so decide on an image that expresses who you are. Are there symbols or mottos that are important to you? Think of quirky things that could be included. If you love classical music, art, rainbows, or flowers, consider featuring these in your labels to develop a personalized label that your friends and family will love.

STORING YOUR BOTTLES

Not all wines are intended to be stored for a long time. Many white and rosé wines should be consumed while they are still young, although they can be stored for a short while. It's essential to store wine in such a way that its quality is preserved.

Some bottles are intended to be stored horizontally, while others are stored upright. When a bottle is stored on its side, the wine and cork meet. This keeps the cork moist and prevents oxygen from entering the wine. The aging process is gradual, so the wine develops its complete range of flavors and aromas. When a bottle is stored upright, the cork is not in contact with the wine. The cork dries out and air enters the bottle. The wine ages more quickly and deteriorates over time. For wines that are aged in the bottle, such as red wines, horizontal storage is essential. If a wine is to be consumed while it is relatively young, it will be stored upright.

It's important to follow wine storage recommendations because wines age more slowly when they are stored at lower temperatures. If it's a red or fortified wine, this ensures that the wine will still be enjoyable in a few years. Temperature and humidity affect the cork's moisture levels, so more oxygen might enter the wine. Dried-out corks won't preserve your wine and allow it to age gracefully.

Avoid exposing the bottles to artificial light or sunlight during storage. Light reduces the wine's longevity and aging capacity. It's also important to ensure that the wine doesn't shake so any sediment can settle. This is particularly important for red wines.

Besides orienting the bottle correctly, the relative humidity needs to be kept constant to maintain the integrity of natural cork. Ensure the wine is stored in an odor-free environment, as corks allow some air into the wine. You don't want unpleasant odors contaminating your wine over time. Don't store onions or garlic near your wines or use paint and solvents near them.

Don't store wine on top of the fridge, as it vibrates and your bottles might fall off and smash. It's also very hot. Rather, invest in a wine fridge that is specially designed to store wine in optimal conditions. These can be adjusted to the correct temperature and will keep the wine at the right humidity. Keeping your wine in a separate fridge will prevent it from becoming contaminated with food odors.

Recork opened wines soon after drinking and ensure that they are properly corked. Wrap the cork in wax paper, as this makes it easier to slide back into place. This will ensure that the leftover wine lasts a little longer. You can also refrigerate the wine.

Storage Guidelines for Different Wine Types

Wine Type	Temperature	Humidity	Storage Position	Other Considerations
Red wines	12 °C–18 °C (55 °F–65 °F)	70%–80%	Horizontal	Avoid vibrations to enable any sediment to settle.
White wines	7 °C–12 °C (45 °F–55 °F)	70%–80%	Upright	Protect from sunlight and artificial light; light degrades the wine.
Sparkling wines	7 °C–12 °C (45 °F–55 °F)	70%–80%	Upright	Avoid temperature fluctuations to maintain the fizz.
Fortified wines (e.g., sherry, port, etc.)	12 °C–18 °C (55 °F–65 °F)	70%–80%	Upright	Protect from artificial light and sunlight to maintain wine quality (Berigan, 2023).

WHY STORE BOTTLED WINES?

Nearly all wines produced are intended to be consumed relatively soon after bottling, often almost immediately. However, there are other wines, often termed vintage wines, which are intended to be aged in the bottle. Such wines can be kept for upwards of 20 years (Michelman, 2021). Wines aged for such lengths of time come into their own later in life, not unlike human beings. They display a complex profile of delicious aromas and flavors that simply don't exist in younger wines. It's as though the wine reveals its softer, more complex heart. Fruity flavors become less prominent, while earthy, spicy, and savory notes come to the fore. For example, the tartness of a Chardonnay might soften to reveal hidden notes of yellow plum and honey, while a Pinot Noir might evolve from more astringent raspberry and cherry to gentler violets and cassis.

As wine ages, it changes chemically, thanks to the action of volatile organic compounds, alcohol esters, and phenols. These changes affect the wine's color, aromas, and flavors. In general, the wine becomes more mellow, and its character alters. Scientists who have studied wine aging attribute vintage wine's highly developed flavors to something called polymerization, when the tannins bind together and float to the bottom of the bottle (Michelman, 2021). In general, the wine mellows out. It's not an exact process and means that just the right amount of oxygen needs to diffuse through the cork, so the wine doesn't become hopelessly oxidized. It has to be stored in exactly the right conditions, too. Some cellars specialize in vintage wines, which are sought-after for special occasions and commemorative anniversaries.

Not all wines are suitable for prolonged aging but some, such as Cabernet Sauvignon, Chardonnay, Pinot Noir, and certain champagne vintages, improve considerably with long-term aging. As for the grapes, the main ones used for creating vintage wines are Cabernet Sauvignon, Chardonnay, Nebbiolo, and Syrah. The truth is that there are endless other varieties, from Riesling to Grenache, that can create wines of this nature when left in the capable hands of talented, experienced winemakers. The aging potential of a wine also depends to some degree on the place where the grapes were grown and the climatic conditions.

The good news is that you can age your wines at home without investing over $100,000 in a bespoke wine cellar if you take special care to create the right conditions. You can do this in a basement with a stable temperature in the right range or a dedicated wine fridge. At home, you can probably age your wine for around five to ten years (Michelman, 2021). While not quite a vintage wine, you'll notice a considerable change in its aromas and flavors. Alternatively, you can take the wine to a dedicated wine storage company that will keep it in their cellars at precisely the right conditions until you wish to retrieve it.

While bottling and storing your wine can take it to the next level, sometimes things don't always go as planned. In the next chapter, you'll find out how to troubleshoot common problems when making homemade wines.

8

WHEN THINGS GO SOUR

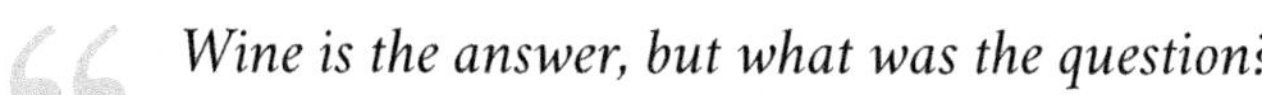

> *Wine is the answer, but what was the question?*
>
> — ANONYMOUS

> *The best way to learn about wine is by drinking.*
>
> — ALEX NICHINE

Not all your winemaking attempts will be trouble-free. In this chapter, you'll find out how to spot potential problems and rectify them. The aim is to turn these stumbling blocks into stepping stones, so you can become a resilient winemaker.

PREVENTION IS BETTER THAN CURE

Making wine can be a very rewarding and interesting experience. There are a few things you can do to prevent problems from occurring, especially if you are a new winemaker (David A. 2021; Time, 2015):

- It's essential to have the right equipment, especially if you want good results. Don't grab an assortment of kitchen utensils and buckets and hope for the best.
- Use quality grapes and ingredients, as well as the best equipment you can afford. This will ensure that your wine production is optimal.
- Make sure that your equipment, utensils, and surfaces are properly cleaned and sanitized before you do anything wine-related. While cleaning simply eliminates any visible dirt and residues, sanitizing means using a sanitizer such as sodium metabisulfite to eliminate all bacteria. Never skimp on this and use recommended products.
- Follow the instructions. These are there to guide you. Use recipes from trusted sources or follow the guidelines that came with your wine starter kit.
- Yeast needs to be handled carefully and used correctly to ensure successful winemaking, as it's a key ingredient in fermentation. Make sure it's at the right temperature when you sprinkle it into your mixture so you get the desired results. If the liquid is too hot, the yeast can be killed off. Don't stir the mixture when adding yeast, as this can be detrimental.
- It can be exciting to see whether your wine is ready, but taking off the airlock too frequently can allow too much oxygen into the fermentation. This can make it less stable and also enable detrimental bacteria to enter the tank, which can cause spoilage. Wine is not completely sterile, so it's best to leave it alone during fermentation.
- Top off your wine to ensure that there isn't too much headspace, as this will allow oxygen to get into your wine.
- Exercise patience. Allow the yeast enough time to turn the fruit sugars into alcohol and for the flavors and aromas to

develop during fermentation. Transferring the wine too early can negatively affect its taste.

- Remember to add sulfite to prevent wine spoilage.
- When adding clarifying agents to your wine at the end of the process, remember to stir and continue stirring until everything is well incorporated.

THREE STEPS FOR TROUBLESHOOTING

When your winemaking isn't going according to plan, don't panic. Follow the procedure below to resolve the problem:

Identify the Problem

This is the first step. Your fermentation might have turned sluggish or become stuck. The wine could smell like vinegar or nail polish remover. There might be signs of oxidation. It could be too fizzy, have deposits on the bottom, or be too sweet.

Determine Possible Causes

Having identified the problem, you need to work out what's causing it. Sluggish or stuck fermentations could be caused by temperatures that rose too high or dropped too low, high sugar or alcohol levels, too much sugar, lack of yeast nutrients, and too little yeast or oxygen.

Take Corrective Action

Just because you've encountered a problem with the winemaking process or the wine itself doesn't necessarily mean that you need to discard it and start again. There are things you can do to rescue the situation.

TROUBLESHOOTING TIPS

In this section, you will find out about common winemaking problems, together with tips for resolving them and ensuring they don't happen in the future.

Stuck Fermentation

What do you do if your fermentation becomes very sluggish or stops altogether? Below are a few tips as to what to do if this happens (Dominowski, 2016):

- If you didn't wait 24 hours after adding the potassium metabisulfite (sulfite), then it could have killed your yeast. Add fresh yeast and nutrients and start the fermentation again. Incidentally, it's not advisable to skip the sulfites, especially if you are a beginner, as this kills off wild yeasts and other unwanted elements in your ferment.
- Ensure that the temperature of the must remains between 21 °C and 30 °C (70 °F and 85 °F). Gently stir the must to keep the temperature in the fermenter constant. If this doesn't work, you could lower clean, sanitized, and sealed jugs of warm water into the must (sanitize the string, too). Stir gently. Fermentation should begin within a day and continue generating its own heat.
- Always use fresh yeast. To test its freshness, make a starter by adding fresh yeast to a few cups of must heated to the temperature the yeast type prefers. Adding some yeast nutrients to the starter will help. Once fermentation starts, pour the starter onto the top of the must but don't mix it in. It may take a few hours for the starter to activate, so wait until it does before adding it to the must. Don't wait too long, though, or the yeast

could use up all the nutrients in the starter and you'll need to begin again.

- There are usually plenty of nutrients for the yeast when fermentation starts but you can add additional nutrients to improve the process. If fermentation slows down after 48 hours, add some yeast energizer (not yeast nutrients).
- During primary fermentation, oxygen is essential, so make sure there is room at the top of your fermenter—or that the lid is on loosely to allow oxygen in while carbon dioxide escapes. Punch down the must cap with the plunger and add yeast energizer. If you are plunging the cap on your must several times a day, you should have sufficient oxygen.
- Your pH level might be too high or low. Aim for a pH of 3.3.
- Ensure that the alcohol level is not too high, as this inhibits the action of the yeast. Maintain alcohol levels at 12% to 14%.
- To keep sugar levels balanced, use good, fresh yeast, ensure that you are using good-quality grapes (avoid high-acid varieties), and do not add sugar to the must.

Unusual Wine Colors

During winemaking, you might notice some undesirable color changes. Here's how to ensure a good wine color and maintain it (Dominowski, 2016):

- Red wine can sometimes be too pale, especially if you are making it from grape juice. Grape skins create the color, so if you don't use them, then the wine will be lighter.
- If the wine turns lighter as it ages, this could be because you filtered out the sediment too meticulously—this

removes the tannins, which affects the color. Use grape varieties that provide good, rich color. If the color has already faded, you might need to blend it with a darker wine. Remember to add more grape skins next time.

- If the wine turns brownish and smells like sherry, then too much oxygen entered it during secondary fermentation or storage. This can also happen if too little sulfite was added during aging. Lightly oxidized white wines can be treated with a fining agent and sulfite before filtering. Lightly oxidized red wines should be left as they are. Unfortunately, there's little you can do about this. If the wine is still salvageable, you can use it for cooking. If the oxidization is severe, you will need to discard it.

Off-Aromas

If the wine smells like burned matchsticks or sulfur, this either means that there was too little yeast in the mixture or too much potassium metabisulfite was added. Try doing vigorous aeration while racking the wine. Some winemakers might suggest adding hydrogen peroxide. Don't do it! While it will break down into oxygen and water, it's a powerful oxidizer that could intensify the problem.

The wine might have a rotten-egg smell, which means it contains too much sulfite or hydrogen sulfide. The wine could also have been starved of oxygen during aging; wine needs tiny amounts of oxygen at this stage. Should you not rack the wine sufficiently, it sits too long on its lees. This makes it smell bad, as do incorrect fermentation temperatures. Some strains of yeast are inclined to produce hydrogen sulfide, so avoid using them. You can resolve mild cases by racking and aerating the wine. Don't add copper sulfate to the batch, as it is poisonous when ingested. Rather, try treating the wine with activated carbon.

Yeasty smells almost always mean that the wine wasn't racked early enough. The dead yeast cells in the lees produce hydrogen sulfide and a substance called mercaptan, which is harmless but smells very pungent. Try racking your wine again, but if the smell persists, the batch cannot be saved.

Odors of vinegar, acetone, or nail polish mean that either the wine oxidized or the bacteria that create vinegar (acetobacter) have taken over. This is also called volatile acidity (VA). Unfortunately, the wine won't be drinkable. If you catch this early enough—when the vinegary smell is still very slight and there is a white film at the top of the fermenter—you can try floating it off by injecting some good wine beneath the film. Be very careful to not mix the film into the wine, as this will make things worse. You won't be able to spoon it off. Filter the wine and rack it over some potassium metabisulfite and lysozyme. Bottle the wine immediately. If it still smells vinegary, you will need to dispose of it.

Other Problems

Cloudy wine can be caused by (Dominowski, 2016):

- improper racking
- bottling while the fermentation is still in progress
- failure to add pectic enzyme

If the wine is still in its aging vessel, you can add more pectic enzyme. Wait a few days and fine the wine with bentonite. Wait a few more days and then rack it.

A sour milk taste means that undesirable bacteria entered the wine. Incorrectly sanitized equipment is usually the culprit. You can try sulfiting the wine. If this makes it drinkable, then drink it soon because the situation won't improve.

A strong barnyard smell coming from a barrel or your wine indicates that it has been infected by Brettanomyces yeast or "Brett." You can try sulfiting the wine, followed by stabilization and filtration. If this happens in a barrel, you will need to discard the wine and stop using the barrel forever.

Bubbly, carbonated wine contains residual carbon dioxide, which means the wine was either improperly degassed or was bottled while malolactic fermentation was still in progress. MLF could also have begun spontaneously in the bottle. If bottled wine tastes good apart from the bubbles, then decant it and allow the bubbles to dissipate before serving. Alternatively, degas the wine by racking or stirring it or using a vacuum pump. You could also just allow the fermentation to complete.

Wine that smells and tastes musty and moldy—like wet dogs, dank basements, or soggy newspapers—most likely has a compromised cork. Fortunately, this means that only that bottle and not your entire batch is affected. Make a crumpled ball of sticky plastic wrap and stuff it into a jug or decanter. Splash-pour the wine over it and wait a few minutes before transferring the wine into a clean container. The culprits (mercaptans) will cling to the polyethylene in the wrap, leaving the wine behind. If it's any consolation, this happens in commercial wineries, too.

Unusually bitter-tasting wine might have absorbed too much tannin from the grape seeds and stems. This can also occur during barrel aging. Fine the wine with egg whites or gelatin. Alternatively, blend it with a less tannic wine or reduce the tartaric acid to balance out the wine.

Your wine might have crystal deposits at the bottom; these can sometimes be mistaken for glass shards and are called wine diamonds. They are actually tartrate crystals and indicate that the wine was not cold-stabilized. Rack the wine. You can then either cold-stabilize it or add metatartaric acid to it.

There is such a thing as storing wine for too long, in which case, it will be past ideal drinking. Storage conditions also affect how the wine ages. Such wines usually exhibit faded color with little character, structure, and freshness. However, this can be subjective. An aged Bordeaux, for example, will soften from ruby to garnet, and the wine's flavor notes will change from fruity to tobacco or cedar. Let your taste buds guide you as to whether the wine is drinkable or not.

Wines can also develop cooked tastes. Red wines that are normally stewed or roasted will develop prune or raisin flavors. Whites will turn brown, nutty, and sherry-like. Prolonged heat exposure or temperature spikes can easily cook a wine. They are often oxidized, too. If the cork has dislodged from the bottleneck, this is a good indication that heat has expanded the air inside. Use it as a braising liquid if the cooked flavors aren't too unpleasant.

Red wines can sometimes develop sedimentary deposits at the bottom or side of the bottle, which are nothing to worry about. This indicates that the wine has aged correctly and will have optimal flavor and texture. Decant your wine before serving.

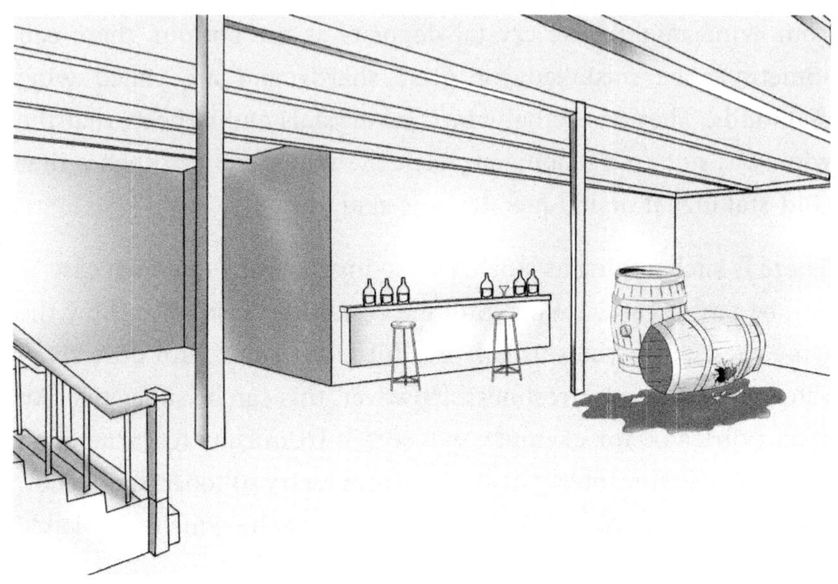

AN OUNCE OF PREVENTION

There are several things you can do to avoid experiencing the wine faults mentioned in this chapter.

Sound winemaking practices help to prevent wine faults, while strict sanitation and cleanliness are essential. All your equipment, vessels, and utensils should be properly cleaned and sanitized before use and thoroughly cleaned afterward.

Use good, healthy grapes that are not rotten, diseased, or infected with fungi. Sort them before use to root out any unwanted debris or compromised grapes. This also reduces the likelihood of detrimental microbes entering your winery.

In addition, ensure that you always (*Wine Faults Series*, 2020):

- add sulfur dioxide during crushing at the rate of 30 to 50 milligrams per liter for clean fruit to reduce the presence of potentially harmful microbes ending up in your wine.

- check that the molecular levels of sulfur dioxide are maintained at 0.8 milligrams per liter.
- keep your tanks and vessels full so there are no air pockets where oxygen can creep in to oxidize your wine.
- blanket vessel headspace with inert gasses such as argon or carbon dioxide.
- check the lids, gaskets, and gauges on variable capacity tanks.
- use tight filter pads when clarifying your wine to reduce bacterial populations.
- do a final filtration using a sterile membrane of 0.45 microns just before bottling.

Preventing Common Wine Faults: Quick Reference Guide

Wine Fault	**Specific Preventative Methods**
Brettanomyces (Brett)	• Monitor the residual sugar levels in your wine during fermentation to ensure that the fermentation completes. • When topping up vessels and barrels, ensure that the wine you are using is not infected. • Ensure adequate sulfur dioxide levels before storage • Smell, taste, and test the wine before using it for topping up your wines.
Cork taint	• Avoid using corks that have been bleached. • Don't use bleach (not even diluted) in vessels, utensils, or production areas, not even for cleaning. • Do not soak corks in sulfur dioxide solutions, as this can compromise their ability to allow tiny amounts of oxygen into the wine during storage. A total lack of oxygen may produce musty or moldy aromas. • Find out what quality control measures are used by cork producers and use synthetic corks or screwcaps if you are unsure.
Spoilage by lactic acid bacteria (LAB)	• Monitor the fermentation to ensure that it proceeds evenly and rapidly, reaching dryness. • Maintain the pH of the wine at 3.6 or less. • With white wine must, reduce suspended solids by cold settling. • Rack as soon as possible following fermentation to reduce the nutrients available to the yeast. • Use tight filter pads when clarifying wine to filter out potentially detrimental bacteria.
Geranium tint (another form of LAB spoilage)	• Avoid stuck fermentations, as this can encourage the growth of LAB. • Use the correct amounts of sulfur dioxide. • Rack early and do sterile filtration to reduce bacterial populations. • Use the appropriate amount of potassium sorbate that contains 74% sorbic acid, as this will inhibit the growth of LAB. • Once the wine has been inoculated with sorbic acid, bottle it within 1–2 days.

Hydrogen sulfide	• Ensure that the entire fermentation is properly managed. • Regularly measure the yeast assemblage nitrogen (YAN) to determine the nutrients present in the juice or must. • Add balanced yeast nutrients as needed. • Ensure that the yeast receives sufficient oxygen during the growth phase (24 hours after inoculation). • Use commercial yeast strains that don't produce hydrogen sulfate.
Oxidation	• Use clean fruit that are not affected by Botrytis or rot. • Add sulfur dioxide in the recommended doses for your wine pH at crushing, aging, and bottling. • Regularly top up the wine to avoid too much headspace. In carboys, leave no more than 1.9 centimeters (¾ inch) head space between the wine and the cap. • Avoid exposing the wine to the air. • Don't stir the wine when transferring it between vessels. • When transferring wine, fill the receiving vessel with an inert gas such as argon or carbon dioxide to avoid oxygen entering the vessel. • If bulk wine is to be aged for a very long period, ensure that no oxygen reaches the liquid.
Tartrate crystals	• Chill the wine to encourage the formation of potassium bitartrate crystals so the wine can be racked or filtered to remove them. • The pH of the wine will change when this is done. Oxygen is more prevalent at lower temperatures, so use an inert gas to protect the wine before starting to remove the crystals. • You can use commercial products to prevent this, such as carboxymethylcellulose, mannoprotein, gum arabic, or polyaspartate. Be sure to follow the manufacturer's instructions.
Protein stability and protein haze	• Heat separates out proteins, so do a heat test before bottling to see whether there are any proteins in the wine that might cause haze. • Cool the wine for at least three hours overnight to give the proteins time to aggregate. • Use bentonite clay to stabilize the wine and follow the manufacturer's directions for preparation. Do not empty the slurry into drains, as it may block them.

Refermentation	When both alcoholic and malolactic fermentation have completed, do the following: • Rack the wine. • Ensure that sulfur dioxide levels are at least 0.8 milligrams per liter of molecular sulfur dioxide based on pH. Larger doses are added early in the winemaking process with smaller adjustments made later. • Avoid adding several smaller, less effective doses of sulfur dioxide throughout the winemaking and storage processes. • Sweeten wines 1–2 weeks before the bottling date. • Sterile filter wines for storage if required. • Store the wine in a cool place (below 12 °C or 54 °F). • Store your wines with minimal oxygen exposure. • Store them dry, if fermented to dryness, even if you will sweeten them before bottling. • Do not store for too long (*Wine Faults Series*, 2020).

Once you've made a good batch of wine, it's time to share it with family and friends. The next chapter will inspire you with ideas for sharing your wine. You can throw dinner parties, have home wine tastings, give your wine away as gifts, and plenty more.

9

SHARING AND ENJOYING YOUR WINE

> *Wine makes every meal an occasion, every table more elegant, every day more civilized.*
>
> — ANDRÉ SIMON

> *Drinking good wine with good food in good company is one of life's most civilized pleasures.*
>
> — MICHAEL BROADBENT

Your winemaking projects create an ideal opportunity for you to share your efforts with others, so your wines have broader appeal. In this chapter, you will find some ideas for appreciating, sharing, and gifting your wine.

WINE TASTING

While you can do wine tasting on your own, it is much more fun if you get a few wine-loving friends to join you. You'll also find out more about your wine, as everyone's palate is slightly different. Below are a few quick tips for getting the most out of your wine tasting (Moore, 2023; *How to Taste and Assess Wine,* 2023):

- Always serve your wines at the correct temperature. If they're too cold, they'll hide their flavors and aromas. Wines that are too warm might taste alcoholic and jammy. Put white wines in the refrigerator about 20 minutes before tasting and take reds out 20 minutes before tasting.
- Avoid strong smells, such as cooking smells, perfume, and other scents that could interfere with the wine's aromas.
- Don't rush the process. Relax, allow the wine to rest in the glass to release more of its flavors and aromas, and enjoy the company. You'll get more out of your wine-tasting experience.
- Taste related wines so you can recognize the nuances between different regions. See how your blend compares to other similar blends. Include a few overseas wines for fun if you have the budget.

What You'll Need

If you're making your own wines, you've probably attended wine tastings before. However, there are a few things to bear in mind if you're hosting your own (Moore, 2023):

- Wine glasses are essential. You don't necessarily need separate ones for red and white, but they should be clean and able to hold at least 1.5 ounces of wine comfortably, with enough space for swirling.

- A white tablecloth or white paper beneath the glasses will make it easier to examine the color of the wine.
- It's best to do a wine tasting in daylight or neutral lighting.
- Serve white and rosé wines at 7 °C to 10 °C (44.6 °F to 50 °F) and reds at 12 °C to 18 °C (53.6 °F to 64.4 °F).

Assessing the Wine

Take notes and work methodically. Keep a file of your wine-tasting notes or use an app to store them. Use a flavor wheel to develop your vocabulary of wine flavors. Be aware of scents like lavender or blackcurrant jam, so you can identify them again. Don't feel intimidated if you smell something others don't. If the wine smells like cheese to you, say so. Trust your instincts. If you're not smelling anything, then rest awhile. Your nose might be tired or the wine might need to rest a bit longer to yield its secrets.

Tasting the Wine

Wine tasting can be divided into four components:

- look (appearance)
- smell (aromas)
- taste (flavors)
- description or score

Appearance

Pour a small amount of wine into your glass. Hold it against a white background and tip the glass slightly backward so the wine is at an angle. You can then assess its clarity and color density.

If the wine is hazy with hints of brown, it might have a tainted cork or have oxidized. If it's clear and only slightly cloudy, then it could be organically produced and unfiltered. Should the wine be translucent and the edges water-like, then you can expect the wine to have a more delicate, lighter flavor. Wines with deep, dense colors are more likely to be full-bodied, higher in alcohol, and have a rich mouthfeel and bold flavor. In red wines, a denser color indicates that it contains more tannins.

The color will tell you something about the wine's flavors. A ruby red wine might indicate a younger wine with fruitier flavors, while a garnet-colored red wine will be older, tasting of nuts, leather, and toast.

White wines should be lemon-green, gold, or lemon-colored. Young wines from warmer climates will have more golden colors. Older wines will appear darker than younger ones.

Rosé wines will be pink, salmon, or peach-orange. The color depends on how long the grape skins remained in the must. These wines usually develop orangey hues as they age.

Red wines are usually purple, ruby, or garnet. Like rosé wines, their color will be darker if the grape skins remained in the must for longer. Red wines tend to lose color as they age.

You might see droplets or tears inside your wine glass after swirling. These are called wine "legs" and have nothing to do with the quality of the wine. Several things affect the development of wine legs—high alcohol content, high amounts of residual sugars in sweet wines, or the temperatures of both the room and the wine.

Aromas

Our sense of smell is closely related to our sense of taste, and taste is actually 80% smell. Our brains remember scents and fragrances for up to a year, while our olfactory senses renew themselves once a month (*How to Taste and Assess Wine,* 2023). Besides sniffing your wine, make a mental note of your surroundings, the people you are with, and the general ambience, as this will help you recall the aromas if you encounter them again.

Lift the glass to your nose and take a quick sniff. Continue taking quick sniffs in between slightly longer inhales and exhale out of your mouth. This is how sommeliers do it. Quick sniffs will continuously introduce the aromas to your olfactory senses, while longer inhales bring the scent further into your palate. There are two things to consider (*How to Taste and Assess Wine,* 2023):

1. The intensity of the wine indicates how aromatic it is. Start by holding your glass about 10 inches from your nose and gradually move it toward your nose until you can smell the wine. If you can already smell it from 10 inches away, then the wine is very intense. If your nose is almost in the glass before you can smell it, then the wine is considered very light. Quality wines will be more intense than cheaper, mass-produced wines.
2. What can you smell? Refer back to Chapter 6 for the different descriptions of a wine's aromas and flavors. Begin by identifying one broad aroma, such as red fruits. Then, narrow it down to strawberries or cherries. White wines will usually have citrussy notes, while red wines will generally remind you of red, black, or blue fruits. After this, try and identify other notes, such as flowers, herbs, and earthiness. Spicy notes occur when the wine was aged

in oak barrels. The more aromas you can identify, the more complex the wine.

The aromas of the wine can also tell you (Moore, 2023):

- what grapes were used.
- the region where the wine was produced and whether the climate was cool or warm.
- how old the wine is.
- whether it was aged in oak.
- whether the wine has any faults.

Flavors

Now, it's time to taste the wine. Take a small sip so it doesn't overwhelm your taste buds and swirl it around your mouth. This means that it will encounter your entire palate and all your taste buds. You'll also get a good idea of the wine's mouthfeel, especially if it is a red wine. It's essential to do this even if you intend to spit out the wine when you are finished tasting it.

Assess six things when tasting wine (*How to Taste and Assess Wine,* 2023):

1. Is the wine sweet or dry? If the wine is very fruity, your taste buds might fool you into thinking it's sweet. One way to establish this is to hold your nose and dip your tongue in the wine. Smack your lips. If you still taste sweetness, the wine is sweet. If not, then it's dry. If the flavor is somewhere in between, then it's off-dry.
2. How acidic is the wine? The more acidic it is, the more saliva your mouth will produce. If you tilt your head forward, you can establish how much saliva collects in your mouth. Cool-climate wines are usually more acidic.

3. Now, assess the flavors. Refer to Chapter 6 for possible flavor descriptions. Remember that these might be similar to the wine's aromas. Note how the flavors develop, fade, or reveal something new.
4. Tannins are most often present in red wines, so you can skip this step if you're tasting whites. Swish the wine around your mouth before swallowing it. How does your mouth feel? If it feels very dry, similar to the way it feels after you've drunk a cup of black tea, then the wine is very rich in tannins.
5. The next thing to assess is the body of the wine. Swirl it around your mouth again. Does it feel like water or creamy, like whole milk? High-alcohol wines tend to be full-bodied, but this is not always the case. Tannins and residual sugars also contribute to a wine's body.
6. The final step is to establish what is called the "finish" of a wine—how long its flavors hold before dissipating in your mouth. The flavors should hold for more than three seconds but less than half a minute.

Description and Score

The final step in wine tasting is to decide whether you like a particular wine or not. It could be a fantastic vintage, but if you don't like how it tastes, then that means nothing. Think about the wines you have just tasted. Would you drink them again, recommend them to others, or buy them for a special occasion? Reference your answers to the previous steps to help you make your decision.

Professional wine tasters usually score the wines they taste according to attributes such as structure, balance, and complexity.

WINE TASTING AT HOME

Wine tasting at home can be a fun way to enjoy wine with your friends and relatives. After setting a date and inviting everyone over to your house, it's time to start planning.

Create a Theme

Create a theme for your wine-tasting party. You can (Tarrier, 2022):

- choose a wine variety and taste varietals from different regions.
- choose wines from a particular region.
- pick a style of wine, such as sparkling, and taste different types.
- choose a wine you like and try different vintages.
- use a wine club mixed case for your tasting.

You can also have a blind wine-tasting party. Decant each wine and label the containers discreetly so you know which is which. You can also wrap the wine bottles in newspapers or foil, so the labels can't be seen. Your guests then taste the wines without knowing what they are. This is a great way to learn about your palate, as well as different wines.

You can either buy the wines yourself or ask each guest to bring a bottle or two along. Ensure that they know the theme for the evening.

What You'll Need

Make sure you have enough wine glasses—work on two or three glasses per guest. If you're tasting more wines, simply tip out the wine and reuse the glasses. Don't wash them between tastings, as the water could dilute the wine. Make sure that you have a bucket or container for people who don't want to drink all the wine, so they can empty their glasses into it. You'll also need palate cleansers—crackers or light bread that can be consumed between each glass of wine. Supply glasses of water for this purpose as well. Everyone should have a notepad and pen so they can record their observations.

Make sure you have the right utensils for opening and serving your wine, such as decanters, carafes, corkscrews, coolers, and so on.

As mentioned previously, use a white tablecloth, ensure there's adequate lighting, and avoid using things such as scented flowers and candles. There should be no cooking or food smells in the room. These could interfere with the aromas and flavors of your chosen wines.

Make sure you have enough wine. For small groups, a bottle of each wine you're tasting will be sufficient, but if you are having more than 10 people, you might need more of each (Tarrier, 2022). Prepare the wine properly, ensuring that it has chilled for long enough, has had time to breathe before tasting, and so on.

After the tasting, you can impress your guests by pairing the wines you've just tasted with snacks or even a meal.

WINE PAIRING

This refers to the art of combining different foods with complementary wines. The wine should be matched to different dishes, the idea being to create a superior dining experience. Start with combinations of foods and wines you like. If you don't normally drink white wine, opt for a food and wine combination that you are more likely to enjoy. A quality, mid-priced wine is perfect for most food pairings.

The food and wine should be in harmony, so neither overpowers the other. Aim for balance, where the wine is matched to the most striking feature of the dish, which could be the main ingredient, sauce, or seasoning. For example, a delicate white wine is perfect with grilled fish, while a bold red wine is ideal for enjoying with a hearty lamb casserole.

Flavor profiles for wine pairings include (*Wine Pairing Tips*, 2021):

- alcoholic
- bitter
- acidic
- salty
- fatty
- sweet

Each of these can be used to create flavor combinations. A bitter, tannic wine could tone down sweet foods or fatty dishes, for example.

Types of Wine Pairings

There are two ways to do wine pairings (*Wine Pairing Tips,* 2021):

1. Contrasting wine pairing is when a bitter flavor balances the richness of the other.
2. Congruent wine pairings are when two complementary flavors are combined to amplify one another and create a good balance.

Below is a quick reference guide to get you started:

Wine Type	**Foods**
Dry white	Bread, fish dishes, desserts, and sweet treats
Sweet white	Cheese, desserts, and sweet treats
Sparkling wine	Fish dishes, bread, and cheese
Dessert wine	Bread, desserts, and sweet treats
Medium red	Beef and chicken dishes

Wine and chocolate can be a wonderful combination, but you can't pair just any chocolate with any wine. Try the following (*Wine Pairing Tips,* 2021):

- dark chocolate with Zinfandel or Shiraz
- milk chocolate with Pinot Noir or Merlot
- white chocolate with Riesling or Rosé

Great Wine Pairings to Try

The truth is that you can pair wines with virtually any food. Here are some great tried-and-tested pairings you can enjoy (Food & Wine Editors, 2023):

- Cabernet Sauvignon with red meat
- Champagne with salty foods, even crisps
- Chardonnay with fatty fish or fish in sauce
- Dry rosé with rich, cheesy dishes
- Off-dry Riesling with sweet, spicy dishes
- Pinot Grigio with light fish dishes
- Pinot Noir with earthy flavors—mushrooms, lentils, and even salmon
- Sauvignon Blanc with tangy dressings and sauces
- Syrah with spicy dishes
- Zinfandel with pates, mousses, and terrines

GIFT-GIVING AND WINE EXPERIENCES

What are the best occasions for giving wine? Birthdays, especially milestones, are a good time to give a bottle of wine. Then, there are weddings, graduations, and the birth of a child. It's even better if you've planned ahead and made some of your own wine especially for the happy event. You could even design a bottle label specially for the recipient. When it comes to events such as weddings, you could make wines that will be ready to drink on the happy couple's first anniversary.

One of the classiest ways to give your wine as a gift is by creating a gift basket. This means that you can include other complementary items with the wine. Below is a guideline as to how to make up a gift basket for your wines (*How to Make Your Own Wine Gift Basket*, 2023):

- The wine will be the focal point, so choose one that the recipient will enjoy, as well as one appropriate for the season or occasion.
- The basket will hold all the elements of your gift. While you can opt for customary wicker or rattan baskets, you could use a pretty gift bag, a decorative pail, a fancy gift box, or even a picnic basket. Choose something the recipient could use again.
- Enhance your basket by adding gourmet snacks that pair well with the wine. These include non-perishables like cheeses, chocolate, crackers, jams, nuts, popcorn, and cured meats.
- You might include some wine-related accessories—wine glasses, corkscrews, wine stoppers, wine books, cheese boards, and so on.

- Use filler materials to protect delicate items or to prop them up so the recipient can see them and the display looks good. You can use shredded or crinkled craft paper, Easter grass, or even tea towels or cloth napkins. If your chosen basket or container is very large, you can fill it up halfway with craft paper before working on your display. Arrange the items from back to front, with the larger items at the back and the smaller ones at the front. Alternatively, opt for a center to perimeter arrangement, with the larger items in the middle. Make sure there are no gaps; individually wrapped chocolates or candies are great for filling empty spaces.
- When you're finished, wrap the entire basket in cellophane or a basket bag bunched over the top of the basket. Add a ribbon or a bow and your gift basket is ready.

Other Wine-Related Gift Ideas

Your wine-loving friends might appreciate gifts such as (*The 5 Best Experience Gifts*, 2023):

- a weekend away at a winery
- a home pub crawl
- a mystery picnic with wine
- a home cheese and wine evening
- wine tasting at a fancy bar

Besides being able to give some very special gifts to your friends and loved ones, there's another wonderful aspect to your wine-making journey—and that's growing your own grapes. In the next chapter, you'll discover how to become truly rooted in your passion for wine.

10

GROWING YOUR OWN GRAPES

> *The ultimate goal of farming is not the growing of crops but the cultivation and perfection of human beings.*
>
> — MASANOBU FUKUOKA

> *Loyal to my soil. Never leave the pad without my blessing oil.*
>
> — E-40, YAY AREA

Growing your own grapes enables you to produce wines that are completely homegrown and personalized. Every part of the process, from growing the grapes to bottling and labeling, creates a unique product. This chapter will introduce you to the art of viticulture—growing grapes for winemaking.

Important note: Most of this chapter is aimed at readers wishing to dive deeper into the world of winemaking. If you prefer to buy or source your grapes from third parties, that's okay, too.

Although most grapes in the United States come from California, vineyards have been successfully planted in most other states. An amateur vintner or winemaker can learn a great deal from visiting small vineyards or wineries close to home or found along the way on a road trip. Residents of other countries may be similarly helped by visiting small-scale vineyards and wineries outside the major wine grape growing areas.

CLIMATE AND WEATHER

Weather refers to naturally fluctuating daily weather conditions, while climate describes long-term trends, such as annual temperatures, rainfall patterns, and sunshine over many years. In Bordeaux, for example, rainfall varies significantly between years, which is why most of the region's wines are blends. This means winemakers are not dependent on one season's grape crop, which might be compromised by heavy rains.

Climate is classified according to the average temperatures throughout the growing season, which runs from April to October in the Northern Hemisphere and October to April in the Southern Hemisphere. Climate types preferable for winemaking are as follows (Terrazas, 2021):

Climate Type	Average Temperatures
Hot climate	Over 21 °C (69.8 °F)
Warm climate	18.5 °C–21 °C (65.3 °F–69.8 °F)
Moderate climate	16.5 °C–18.5 °C (61.7 °F–65.3 °F)
Cool climate	Up to 16.5 °C (61.7 °F)

Grapes grow better in places with warm daytime temperatures and cool nights. Warm daytime temperatures ripen the grapes, concentrating their tannins and flavors. Cool overnight temperatures preserve aromas and acidity. Regions with significant temperature changes between night and day produce fresher, more aromatic wines. Spring frosts, together with reduced or excessive rainfall and sunshine, can be detrimental to grapes, negatively affecting bud break, fruit ripening, and sugar or tannin levels. If too little rain falls, irrigation will be needed so the vines don't suffer from heat stress or drought.

Optimal climate types for grape-growing are (Terrazas, 2021):

Climate Type	Description	Grape Types
Continental climate	Normally found inland, these regions have marked temperature differences between the hot and cold seasons. Hot summers are usually followed by frigid falls and winters. Frost may occur during bud break, with lower average temperatures over the growing season, which can affect flowering, fruit set, and ripening.	This climate produces grapes that bud later in spring and ripen in fall.
Maritime climate	Temperatures tend to be moderate to cool, and temperature differences between warm and cold seasons are more uniform. Rainfall occurs all year. Heavy rain in spring and summer can affect flowering, fruit set, and grape health. Grapes may ripen into fall.	Grapes such as Cabernet Sauvignon, which have thick skins, ripen successfully regardless of temperature variations.
Mediterranean climate	There are significant differences in temperature between warm and cold seasons. Warm, dry summers alternate with cool, wet winters.	Wines are often full-bodied with low acidity, higher alcohol, more tannins, and fruity flavors due to the warmer climate.

Local and regional climates determine cultivation practices. Before opting to grow your own grapes, obtain long-term weather data for your region to see whether the climate is suitable. You will also need this information to decide on vineyard orientation, choose grape varieties, and establish what wines you could produce.

Growing Grapes in Other Climates

Can you grow grapes if you live in a country that doesn't lie between the 30th and 50th parallel or if your regional climate isn't suitable for grape cultivation? You can take comfort from knowing that, even in regions with ideal climates and an established reputation for grape cultivation and winemaking, unusual weather can bring heavy frosts at bud break, for example, ruining an entire season's production.

There are indications that subjecting vines to adverse conditions might actually produce better grapes. If grapevines are given exactly what they fancy—plenty of nutrients and water—they often produce substandard grapes. When left to their own devices, vines would far rather produce shoots and leaves than fruit. This is why wild grapes normally bear only occasional bunches of sourish grapes, despite their deceptively luxuriant vines.

Vintners know this and use counterintuitive tactics to get the best out of their vines. They restrict water and nutrient supplies, crowd the plants too near their neighbors, and prune them to the bone. This awakens the vines' survival instincts, so they put more effort into developing fruits in an effort to reproduce themselves out of adversity. They grow deeper roots to find more water and nutrients. Yields might be a little lower, but grape quality is superior. While this approach to grape growing needs to be carefully managed, it demonstrates that conditions don't need to be optimal for your vines to produce quality grapes for winemaking. Consider ice wines, which are harvested when frigid winter weather has frozen the grapes on the vines.

Do your research and see what's possible in your situation. Perhaps you need to consider hardy, cold-climate grapes or one of the new heat-tolerant varieties. You might even find that your property has just the right slope with a microclimate perfect for growing grapes.

Influence of Daily Weather

Daily weather forecasts—air pressure, temperature, humidity, precipitation, wind speed, and wind direction—will determine your routine vineyard activities. For example, certain plant protection products work at specific temperature ranges, while wind speed and direction determine whether you can spray your vines on a specific day. Weather-related information can help to predict vine and grape diseases, so you can take timely preventative action.

You could also invest in your own weather station, as regional ones might be some distance from your location, resulting in inaccuracies. Microclimate weather data obtained from different parts of your vineyard will help you manage the different sections optimally, although this mostly applies to larger vineyards.

SELECTING THE RIGHT GRAPES FOR YOUR REGION

When choosing grape varieties, select ones adapted to your local growing conditions and climate. University websites can provide useful information in this regard. As discussed previously, both the climate and factors responsible for "terroir" mean that the same grape varieties can produce very different wines depending on where they are grown. Some grapes do best in cooler climates, while others prefer warmth.

Cold-Climate Grapes

Grape varieties suitable for cold climates include Chardonnay, Pinot Noir, and Riesling. Ice wines are made by allowing the grapes to freeze on the vine, which concentrates their natural sugars. Riesling and Vidal Blanc are mostly used for ice wines.

Warm-Climate Grapes

Cabernet Sauvignon, Sangiovese, Syrah (Shiraz), and Zinfandel are grape varieties that thrive in warm regions with Continental or Mediterranean climates. While Syrah does well in warm climates, it becomes more fruity when grown in warmer places such as Australia's Barossa Valley or California's Paso Robles region.

PREPARING YOUR VINEYARD

There are several things to consider when starting your own vineyard.

Site Selection

When planning your vineyard, consider the microclimate—the site-specific climate as opposed to the overall local or regional one. The microclimate might encompass a few acres or extend for some miles. Factors influencing microclimates include (Briscoe, 2023):

- temperature
- humidity
- soil type(s)
- proximity to water bodies
- elevation and altitude
- geographical features

These may vary in even a small area or single vineyard. They will influence fruit ripening and harvest times and might create opportunities to produce a signature wine. Microclimates are influenced by regional topography and geography—hills, valleys, plateaus, and distance from the coast. Vineyards on valley floors, for instance, are more likely to experience frost and heavy fog, as cold air tends to sink. This may create a cooler microclimate. Vineyards higher upslope will receive sunshine for longer but can get colder at night due to their elevation. These details will guide your grape variety selection.

Slope

Hillsides are preferable for vineyard cultivation. Although soils are less fertile, this can be beneficial when cultivating grapes. Slopes are less prone to the frosts that might affect bud break in spring, a critical time for growers. Gentle slopes are preferable, as the soils drain better. If there are nearby valleys where cold air collects, this may reduce the chances of frost in the vineyard. Steep slopes make vineyard management difficult, and terracing may be required. This raises start-up costs.

While vineyards can be planted on flat land, this dilutes the intensity of the sunshine, as the sun's rays spread across the site, rather than concentrating on the slope. Drainage may be poorer, depending on the soil type, so plant roots may become too moist or even waterlogged, especially after heavy rains. Vines grow more vigorously on flat lands and need more pruning and canopy management to ensure the development of fruit rather than vegetative growth. On the plus side, it's easier to manage and maintain flat vineyards.

Elevation

Elevation affects vineyard temperatures. At high latitudes, locations at lower elevations are favored, while higher elevations are preferable at lower latitudes. Average annual temperatures generally fall by 0.61 °C per 100 meters (1.1 °F per 330 feet) of elevation (Goldammer, 2021). This creates shorter growing seasons and can increase the likelihood of frost at higher elevations. Particularly when planning vineyards at higher altitudes with cooler climates, it may also be necessary to consider the thermal belt—the band within which there is less likelihood of frost and freezing temperatures, regardless of elevation.

Orientation of the Vineyard (Aspect)

In the Northern Hemisphere, a south-facing vineyard receives more sunshine, while a north-facing one receives less sunlight and is cooler. In the Southern Hemisphere, the opposite applies. Laying out the vineyard to take advantage of maximum sunlight exposure could facilitate earlier bud break, especially in areas with a low possibility of spring frosts.

West-facing slopes are helpful for late-maturing varieties, where the fruit ripens in fall's shorter days and diminishing heat. East-facing vineyards benefit from early morning sunshine, which warms the canopy and soils earlier in the day.

Wind

In some microclimates, wind might affect the vines. In the Petaluma Gap American Viticultural Area (AVA), for instance, the wind blows through a gap in the hills, bringing cooler ocean breezes inland. The grapes have developed thicker skins, darkening wine colors and concentrating tannins and flavors. Winds are a bit of a two-edged sword. While they might cool temperatures down, strong winds may break vines and shoots, dry out soils, or bring salt spray from the ocean that might burn plants.

Humidity

If the vineyard is close to forests, rivers, or large water bodies, such as lakes, dams, or the ocean, this can raise humidity levels, potentially reducing climate extremes. The diffused reflection of sunlight off water surfaces, combined with direct sunshine, can hasten fruit ripening.

Previous Crops

Before purchasing or planting your land, try and establish what previous crops were grown there, together with the agricultural practices used. Below are some difficulties you might experience due to former crop cultivation (Strafne, 2019):

- Some agricultural chemicals persist in the soil for a long time and may damage your vines.
- Fungal diseases sometimes occur in association with trees like oaks. Allow a recently cleared forest to lie fallow for at least a year—and preferably three to five years—after clearing to reduce the incidence of detrimental fungi in the soil. These fungi often associate with plant roots and may persist on remnant roots. They could negatively impact your vines if you cultivate the land too soon.
- Pest nematodes can be a problem in some agricultural soils. Have your soils tested to determine the presence of detrimental nematodes before planting.
- Some soils may contain excessive nitrogen from previous applications. They may need to lie fallow to allow the nitrogen to degrade. Alternatively, avoid planting vines in those spots.
- Aluminum toxicity can be problematic in some soils. Avoid growing your vines in soils with a low pH (acidic soils). Alternatively, you will need to raise pH levels. Monitor the pH throughout the life of your vineyard, as naturally acidic soils tend to revert to type.

PLANT NUTRIENTS

Plants, including grapevines, require 14 essential nutrients, which are obtained from the soil or fertilizer applications. These are (Rosen, 2014):

Primary Macronutrients	**Secondary Macronutrients**	**Micronutrients**
Nitrogen (N)	Sulfur (S)	Zinc (Zn)
Phosphorus (P)	Magnesium (Mg)	Boron (B)
Potassium (K)	Calcium (Ca)	Iron (Fe)
		Manganese (Mn)
		Copper (Cu)
		Molybdenum (Mo)
		Nickel (Ni)
		Chlorine (Cl)

Nutrients need to be present in the soil in sufficient quantities to be taken up by plants. The ability of the soil to release these nutrients can be affected by soil composition, pH, soil texture (quick-draining soils such as sand leach nutrients faster, for example), the amount of organic matter present, and how the land was previously managed.

Grapes are a perennial crop, so the plants will be cultivated for several years across all seasons. Once the vines are planted, nutrients can be applied only to the soil surface to avoid harming the plants' root systems. For some amendments (any material added to the soil to improve its physical or chemical properties), surface applications have little effect.

SOIL ANALYSIS AND PREPARATION

Before preparing the lands, you will need to find out about the status of the soil. Soil testing and analysis will determine the soil pH (acidity or alkalinity), how much organic matter is present (OM%), and the concentrations of key plant nutrients such as nitrogen, potassium, and phosphorus, together with macronutrients such as boron, copper, and zinc. Conduct soil tests a year before planting, as this will give you time to improve the soil by increasing its organic matter and balancing the nutrients.

The analysis will indicate problems such as salinity and acidity. Once dissolved in water, minerals can be absorbed only by plant roots. Soil pH indicates how efficiently your plants will be able to take up these dissolved nutrients. The ideal pH for vineyards is between 6.0 and 7.0. If the pH is too low (i.e., too acidic), then the vines won't be able to take up certain nutrients, while others, such as aluminum and manganese, could be absorbed too easily, potentially reaching toxic levels in the plants (Goldammer, 2021).

Sandy soils have large pores between soil particles and drain rapidly, so nutrients leach out easily after irrigation or rainfall. Where sands are water-repellent, water movement is slow, and there are fewer nutrients in the deeper levels of the soil. Low levels of organic matter reduce soil fertility.

The soil sample needs to reflect the soil throughout the vineyard to ensure an accurate analysis and that the correct actions are taken. The best time to take soil samples is in the fall. Avoid taking samples during or after a drought or when the soil is frozen, snow-covered, or flooded.

When the vineyard is established, soil testing should be done once every three years. This will confirm plant tissue analysis and establish the soil's pH, as well as its nutrients (Klodd & Rosen, 2021).

How to Take Soil Samples (Unplanted Vineyards)

Soil should be taken randomly but uniformly across the entire vineyard. Ensure that each sample has the same soil texture and color, was subjected to the same agricultural treatments, and has the same cropping history. If the topography is varied, you will need samples taken at different heights.

Divide the entire area into sections with the same soil texture, organic matter, cropping history, slope, and drainage. Samples can be taken in a random or zigzag fashion, but the entire block must be covered.

A single sample should not represent more than 20 acres on flat land and 5 acres on sloping land. Each sample should contain at least 10 to 15 sub-samples taken throughout the sample area. Collect samples from the top 20 centimeters (8 inches) of the soil. This is the topsoil that contains the organic matter and most of the nutrients. For new vineyards, include samples taken 20 to 40 centimeters (8 to 16 inches) below the soil surface as well (Klodd & Rosen, 2021).

Use a special soil sample tube (profile tool), an auger, or a garden spade. After collection, mix the samples thoroughly in a plastic bucket and place about 500 grams (16 ounces) of the mixture in a generic paper bag (Klodd & Rosen, 2021). Mark the sample clearly with the name of your vineyard, your name, your contact information, and the type of analysis required. The agricultural laboratory will advise you on the correct soil sample collection protocols, as well as the completion of the relevant forms. You will usually need to pay them before they will perform the analysis. Some jurisdictions such as the Cooperative Extension Service in the United States or REQUASUD in Belgium offer subsidized services and advice.

AMENDING YOUR SOIL FOR OPTIMAL FERTILITY

When you have received your soil analysis back from the laboratory, you may find that you need to take steps to correct any problems or imbalances.

Altering Soil pH

If the analysis reveals that your soil pH is too low (below 6.0), raise the pH by applying lime, which also adds calcium and magnesium. There are two types (Rosen, 2014):

1. Dolomitic lime contains magnesium and calcium.
2. Calcitic lime contains mainly calcium.

Lime is normally incorporated into the top 20 to 25 centimeters (8 to 10 inches) of the soil. Do this one year before planting.

Soils derived from limestone most often have high pH, so they are frequently too alkaline. This can cause severe iron deficiencies, resulting in yellow leaves. If your soil pH is over 7.0, this is more difficult to change. Elemental sulfur is normally used but must be applied judiciously. Get professional advice, as application rates vary depending on the type of soil and the amount of organic matter present. If carbonates are present in the soil, it is not advisable to use elemental sulfur. Rather apply iron chelates if your vines develop an iron deficiency (Rosen, 2014).

Macronutrients

Nitrogen

If there is insufficient nitrogen in the soil, your vines won't grow properly. Nitrogen is derived from the air, lightning, and nitrogen-fixing microorganisms in the roots of legumes. Because it moves through the soil, is usually unnecessary to add nitrogen to the soil before planting.

If there is insufficient nitrogen in the soil, the vines will grow poorly, and the leaves will yellow. The grapes will be low in sugar, and they won't have enough nitrogen to feed the yeast during fermentation. On the other hand, excessive nitrogen results in excessive vegetative growth and poor fruit color.

Nitrogen should only be applied in the first and second years after planting. Synthetic (inorganic) nitrogen can be applied soon after planting but only if required. When determining application rates, take into account the nitrogen derived from compost, manures, and leguminous cover crops (e.g., beans, peas, alfalfa, or cover).

Synthetic nitrogen is available in several forms (Rosen, 2014):

- Calcium nitrate increases soil pH and is useful when the soil pH is too low. It is readily available to plants but leaches easily with irrigation or rainfall runoff.
- Urea tends to destabilize when applied to the soil surface, especially when soil pH is on the high side.
- Ammonium sulfate reduces soil pH and converts to nitrate, which is easily absorbed by plants. It is more stable than urea.

Phosphorus

This is very immobile in the soil and needs to be added before planting if your soil analysis indicates that this is necessary. Deficiencies may occur on acidic soils with a pH lower than 5.3. Phosphorus deficiencies are rarely a problem for established vines (Rosen, 2014).

If your phosphorus levels are low, you can apply manure or compost in the fall as organic nitrogen sources. Alternatively, apply triple superphosphate or mono-ammonium phosphate. Broadcast these over the soil and incorporate them to a depth of 20 to 25 centimeters (8 to 10 inches) (Rosen, 2014).

Potassium

This nutrient does not move easily through the soil. If your soil analysis indicates that your soil is deficient in potassium, you will need to amend it before planting. Grapes are susceptible to potassium deficiencies, especially when fruiting. This can cause low sugar levels in the fruit. If potassium levels are too high, fruit will be less acidic.

Potassium can be applied to the soil as potassium chloride, potassium sulfate, or potassium magnesium sulfate. Spread them over the soil and incorporate them to a depth of 20 to 25 centimeters (8 to 10 inches) (Rosen, 2014).

Magnesium

If too much potassium has been applied to a sandy soil—which is a situation you might inherit—then your plants might struggle to take up magnesium. To rectify this, apply dolomitic lime if your soil pH is too low (acidic) to bring the pH back to 6.0 or 6.5. Epsom salts can be used if the pH is within normal ranges.

Micronutrients

Micronutrients are usually present in sufficient quantities in soils to meet the needs of plants. If the soil is very sandy or has a high pH, then deficiencies could occur. Grapevines are most likely to be affected by shortages of boron, iron, manganese, and zinc. To maintain adequate micronutrient levels, monitor and manage soil pH.

Using manure as a nutrient source increases the levels and availability of micronutrients in the soil. Foliar fertilizers containing micronutrients can be used after vines are established.

Other Soil Amendments

Three main soil amendments are applied to soils when establishing vineyards and growing grapes (Braum, n.d.).

Gypsum

Gypsum is a calcium salt derived from sulfuric acid that doesn't alter soil pH. When gypsum dissolves in water, it releases calcium and sulfur, both of which benefit soils. The calcium released helps maintain and stabilize soil structure. Well-structured soils deliver sufficient water to the root zone while maintaining good drainage. Plant roots will penetrate the soil more easily as they grow, and the soil is sufficiently aerated, so it supplies air to plant roots. Gypsum is comprised of crystals. If these are too large, the gypsum will take a while to dissolve. When purchasing gypsum for agricultural use, source one with a fine grind (particles under 1 millimeter in diameter). Spread the gypsum evenly when applying.

Compost

This is organic waste broken down by beneficial microbes. Its nutrient content varies depending on the source, as manures generate more macronutrients than green materials. Applying compost provides nutrients that are released gradually to plants. Most compost breaks down within a year, although regular applications result in long-term soil improvement, which increases soil productivity, so fertilizer applications can be reduced. Nitrogen is released when the soil is active, and it is also used when the compost breaks down. This means that the nitrogen in compost is often insufficient for the vines' requirements and needs to be supplemented. A low-nutrient, stable compost is best for augmenting soil organic matter.

Lime

This is the third amendment commonly used in vineyards and has already been discussed in the section dealing with altering pH.

TRELLISING

Before planting your vines, you will need to install a trellising system to support them. Choosing a trellis system depends on several factors, including how fast the vines grow, whether they grow upward or downward, and how the vines are pruned.

The training system you choose is important because it can potentially affect (Judy, n.d.):

- how much shade and sun the grapes receive
- vine balance
- ease of pruning and harvesting
- how much heat rises from the ground toward the fruit
- wind impacts
- frost damage

Trellising Benefits

Photosynthesis (the process by which plants make their food using sunlight and carbon dioxide) occurs in vine leaves, enabling the plants to produce sufficient sugars and other compounds to create quality fruit. Developing canes need light to form the buds that will produce the following year's crop. Effective canopy management, good pruning, and a north-south trellis alignment ensure that plenty of sun reaches the vines. A good trellising system creates a large canopy with two to three leaf layers and minimal shading (Garnet & Read, n.d.). This ensures a quality crop and fruit with high sugar levels.

Grapevines are susceptible to fungal diseases, which can be countered by encouraging good airflow around the vines and canopy. This is facilitated by growing the vines on a trellis. Fruit is unlikely to touch the ground, eliminating soil-borne diseases. It is also easier to weed beneath the plants and to spray the vines with fungicides and insecticides.

Well-designed trellises make harvesting much easier. The trellising system used depends on whether the grapes will be harvested by hand or mechanically.

Trellising Tips

Trellises should be matched to the cultivar's growth habit. Cultivars that grow downward need to be trained along the top wire of the trellis, at least 1½ to 2 meters (5 to 6 feet) above the ground (Garnet & Read, n.d.). The vine reaches the ground at the end of the growing season. The shoots of vines with an upward growth habit are positioned on a mid- or low-wire cane or cordon and then trained upward using catch wires.

The speed with which the vines grow is called vigor. It's necessary to establish this before settling on a trellis system. This is very important: If the vigor is underestimated and the trellis is too small, shading could occur. If vigor is overestimated and the vines are placed too far apart, yields will be lower.

Materials

The foundation of your trellis is the most vital aspect of construction. This is the end-post assembly, which anchors the trellis system, and it's advisable to avoid taking shortcuts. The H-brace system is the most commonly used. Alternatively, the end post is put in at a 15° angle from the vertical with an anchor such as a "dead man." The end post materials need to be sturdy—some growers opt for a 20 centimeters (8 inches) diameter end post (Garnet & Read, n.d.). End posts may consist of steel placed in concrete, concrete posts, old railway line ties, or piping from old pivot irrigation systems. Ensure that your choice is strong enough and won't leach toxins into your vines. Posts will be more stable if they are driven into the ground rather than placed in pre-dug holes.

Line posts hold the trellis system off the ground. Landscape timbers or steel T posts are usually used for this. Bear in mind that even treated landscape timbers eventually succumb to the elements and rot. Steel posts may sink into the ground or bend if the vines are heavy with fruit, especially in strong winds. Fiberglass poles, treated fence posts, and well pipe can also be used.

Don't skimp on the wire. High-tensile, 12-gauge steel wire is essential. If your wires break under a heavy crop load, this can be disastrous. It is almost impossible to repair, you will incur significant costs and need more labor, and your yield may be reduced.

When constructing your trellises, ensure that you have the right tools for the job.

Trellis Types

There are several types of trellis, depending on the cultivar and the pruning method employed.

- Umbrella Kniffin System (KFS)
- High Cordon System (HCS)
- Geneva Double Curtain (GDC)
- Mid-Wire Vertical Shoot Positioning (VSP)
- Fan System
- U or Lyre System
- Scott Henry
- Smart-Dyson
- Smart-Dyson Ballerina

GRAPEVINE CARE AND MAINTENANCE

Irrigation

Like other crops, grapevines need watering to supplement rainfall or during dry periods. The amount of water required depends on their age, the season, what cultivars you are growing, your climate, and soil type.

In the wild, grapes favor dry conditions. However, when they are being grown to produce quality wines, both the quantity and timing of the water they receive are crucial. Wine grapes are relatively drought-tolerant and can manage with just 508 millimeters (20 inches) of water during the entire growing season. Red wine grapes can grow with just 304 millimeters (12 inches) of annual rainfall without any adverse effects (Hansen, 2011). To avoid water stress, most grapevines generally require 635 to 890 millimeters

(25 to 35 inches) of water annually, mainly during spring and summer (*Irrigation in Viticulture*, 2023).

Wine quality improves if the vines are allowed to experience water stress at certain times during the growing season. In countries where grapes are grown in Mediterranean climates with low humidity levels, such as parts of Chile and South Africa's Western Cape, irrigation is needed to supplement natural rainfall or replace it. By contrast, Tuscany receives much of its annual rainfall between April and June, during budding and fruit set when the plants have higher water requirements (*Irrigation in Viticulture*, 2023).

From bud break to bloom, grapes don't need much water, but they do need water from bloom to fruit set for good yields. Most of the vineyard's water requirements are from fruit set to veraison (the onset of grape ripening). Water is taken up by young roots that die quickly, so the plant needs to grow replacements. As the leaf canopy size expands, so do the vine's water requirements. A square meter (10.7 square feet) of canopy will use as much as 2 to 3 liters (½ to ¾ gallon) of water a day due to evaporation and transpiration (when water is pulled from the roots up through the plant to escape through tiny leaf pores called stomata) (Hansen, 2011).

Growers in semi-arid areas who use irrigation have an advantage over those who receive rainfall throughout the growing season. Using irrigation, growers can control exactly how much water is delivered and when to determine canopy size, plant growth, and the size of grape berries.

While some water stress can improve fruit quality, don't go overboard. The vine's shoots and tendrils climb as they grow. If the shoots become longer than the tendrils and the canopy starts shedding leaves, the vine is stressed.

Grapevines' water needs vary between varieties. Some close their stomata to prevent water loss as soon as the water supply reduces so the amount of water in the leaf remains stable. Growth slows. Grape varieties sensitive to water reductions include Cabernet Sauvignon, Grenache, and Tempranillo. Other varieties keep their stomata open and continue growing. These include Chardonnay, Merlot, Sangiovese, Syrah, and Riesling. Red and white grape varieties have different water requirements, with sun exposure and berry size being more important in reds.

Tailor water provision to your particular site and the grape varieties you are growing. The later in the season the vines become water stressed, the better for your crop. If there is insufficient water after veraison and leaves start wilting or dropping off the vines, the fruit will be low in sugar. Reducing water earlier in the growing season increases tannins in the fruit. It is not advisable to reduce irrigation during fruit ripening.

In general, don't reduce irrigation during fruit set and later in the season, as this could negatively affect budding, fruit set, and yields. Providing too much water mid-season can encourage larger berry sizes. During hot, dry seasons, providing more water to white varieties might delay ripening, which can encourage acidity and flavor development.

Overwatering can also be detrimental to vines. When vines become waterlogged, bacteria and fungi in the soil start competing for nutrients. Wet soils are often cold, and when this coincides with the flowering season, it may result in poor fruit set. Fruits require warmth radiating from the ground to promote proper ripening, especially in cold climates. Wet, cold soils might delay ripening. Well-draining soils are preferable for grape cultivation.

Fertilization

From the second year of production, you will need to conduct a leaf sample analysis, which is normally based on the leaf stalk (petiole) of the leaf. This measures the amount of nutrients the plants have taken up from the soil. This is done annually and enables growers to fine-tune their fertilizer programs and make corrections to avoid any negative outcomes. It is also important to monitor soil pH.

Taking Petiole Samples

- Take samples at the same time every year. In the Northern Hemisphere, this is usually from late July to early August.
- Each variety should be sampled separately.
- If your vines are growing on different soil types, collect individual samples for each soil type.
- If different parts of your vineyard received different fertilizer applications, these should be sampled separately.
- Laboratories normally need 100 petioles per sample or 150 to 200 petioles if you have varieties with short petioles. This is to ensure that there is enough material to conduct the required analyses (Domoto, 2013).

Correcting Nutrient Deficiencies

Add nutrients only if your petiole analysis indicates that this is necessary.

Nitrogen

The amount of actual nitrogen required is calculated by determining how much nitrogen will be removed through leaching and fruit picking, as well as how much will be added by organic matter, nitrogen-fixing plants, and lightning. For acidic soils with low pH, nitrates should be applied, as this will help raise the pH. Urea can be used in soils where the pH is optimal, while ammonia should be used in soils with a high pH, as this will tend to lower it. Only apply complete fertilizers if there is a need for all the nutrients (potassium and phosphorus in addition to nitrogen) or nutrient imbalances may result.

Nitrogen is most necessary when the vines are in bloom. You can apply nitrates, which the plants can easily take up, but they are prone to leaching. This nutrient should be applied in the form of urea in early spring, as well as late fall, when growth stops for the season. Ammonia can be used as an alternative. Nitrogen is released very slowly and soil temperatures need to be at least 10 °C (50 °F) (Domoto, 2013). Ammonia might bind to soil particles, although it is less prone to leaching. Manures can be applied post-harvest and once the growing season ends in fall.

Phosphorus and Potassium

If phosphorus levels are low in sandy soils, apply manure in the fall as a nitrogen source. Alternatively, use winery pomace (dried), ammonium mono phosphate, or phosphorus as a foliar feed.

If your petiole analysis indicates a potassium deficiency, you will need to get it into the root zone. A soil test will determine how much will be needed. Test magnesium levels at the same time to ensure that magnesium is not inhibiting the uptake of potassium and that adding potassium to the soil will not reduce the availability of magnesium.

Potassium should be applied to the soil in early spring in the form of potassium nitrate. If the need is identified as a result of a petiole analysis, then apply potassium chloride, potassium sulfate, or potassium magnesium sulfate. Foliar applications may also be needed in addition to soil amendments. Apply potassium early in the season. You can also use straw mulch underneath vines.

Calcium deficiency is not generally a problem in grapes unless they are growing in sandy soils. In this case, apply either lime or gypsum depending on your pH levels. You can use calcium nitrate as your nitrogen source.

Other Nutrients

Magnesium shortages can be an issue, especially if potassium has been over-applied. If the soil pH is low (acidic), you can apply dolomitic lime. Alternatively, if the pH is optimal, apply magnesium oxide together with Epsom salts. Epsom salts should also be applied twice after blooming. Be careful of adding magnesium if you are growing grapes on calcareous or glaciated soils, as this might inhibit the uptake of potassium.

Sulfur is often used in spray programs. If sulfur is below 0.10% according to your petiole analysis, check the soil pH and acidity if necessary. You can also use a fertilizer that contains sulfur in your fertility program. Apply liquid lime sulfur when the vines are dormant, as this will also control anthracnose, a fungal root disease. You can also use sulfur-containing fungicides if your varieties are not sensitive to sulfur.

Boron is important for good fruit set, as it improves pollen tube growth and flower fertilization. Apply small amounts to the soil 4.48 to 6.7 kilograms per hectare (4 to 6 pounds per acre) (Domoto, 2013).

Copper might be low, especially on sandy or alkaline soils. Apply Bordeaux mixture (copper sulfate with hydrated lime) as part of your disease control. Do not apply copper before or just after cold, wet weather, as this will increase its absorption. Too much copper can make the plant light-sensitive and the leaves will burn. Copper also helps to control anthracnose.

Manganese may also be low in sandy or alkaline soils, in which case apply a fungicide containing manganese, such as mancozeb, in your early season disease control program. Manganese might also be high in acidic soils, in which case, apply lime to raise the pH.

Zinc can be low in disturbed, alkaline soils. Apply zinc sulfate and use a zinc-containing fungicide in your early-season disease control program. You can also apply zinc as a foliar spray.

Iron can be low in alkaline and sandy soils. Apply iron chelate as a foliar spray and repeat every 10 to 20 days (Domoto, 2013). Lower soil pH to improve the availability of iron.

Pruning

Pruning is done in winter, after harvesting and when the vines have entered dormancy (*Pruning,* n.d.). Pruning affects the quality and quantity of your harvest, as well as the ultimate health of your vines. Assess and prune every vine individually.

In larger vineyards, machine pruners begin pruning by removing dead wood from the canopy. Thereafter, human pruners complete the job. In the first phase, the previous year's growth is cut back to about 30 to 38 centimeters (12 to 15 inches) from the trunk. The pruning is completed later in the season, when only the fruit-producing shoots will be left. This prevents fungi from entering the vine wood (Young, 2018).

The second round of pruning is done by hand. The canes are reduced to one per spur with only two buds per cane. Each bud will grow into new canes that will bear that season's fruit—two bunches of grapes per cane (Young, 2018).

Two types of pruning are done in vineyards (Garnet & Read, n.d.):

1. Cane pruning retains long canes with 10 to 20 nodes for fruiting.
2. Spur pruning results in shorter, 2- to 6-node canes for fruiting (Garnet & Read, n.d.).

Both methods suit most cultivars and trellis systems. Some cultivars yield more fruit when canes are pruned because the buds 4 to 12 nodes from the base are more productive than the first few nodes. Some cultivars develop several secondary and tertiary buds from canes with short spur pruning (two nodes) encouraging this. Long-spur pruning (six nodes) or cane pruning will prevent this (Garnet & Reed, n.d.).

Managing Weeds

In vineyards, plants and fruits are closer to the ground than they are in orchards. Weed control involves pre-empting problems before they start. Keep the vineyard clean to control weeds without using herbicides. Cover crops planted between rows and mechanical weed control within the rows are the main aspects of organic weed control.

You can also lay black plastic over the area, burying the edges so it doesn't blow away. This process is called solarization and is most effective when the soil is saturated with water and wrapped in two layers of transparent plastic. Clear plastic traps more heat energy than black plastic, and the high moisture content increases the enthalpy of the treated soil. Solarization effectively heats the soil and cooks the weeds and their seeds, so they die. Do this in midsummer, when the days are the longest and warmest. This is an excellent intervention to make before planting but is inappropriate after the vines have been planted. Remove the plastic before planting.

Ensure that weeds are under control before planting the vines, so they don't compete with the new vines for water, nutrients, and light. Before planting, irrigate the area so the weeds germinate. When the weed seedlings appear, till the ground to uproot them. This reduces the weed seed bank in the soil. Repeat this process until the weed population reduces.

Cultivation uproots and buries weeds. Pull them out by hand while they are small or destroy them by slicing them. Carefully turn over the soil to expose weed roots. If your vineyard is small enough, you can remove weeds with a hoe.

Covering the soil with mulch starves the weeds of light. The larger the mulch pieces, the deeper the layer needs to be. Organic mulches should be at least 10 centimeters (4 inches) thick, but there are some drawbacks to using them (Roncoroni et al., 2015):

- They break down over time and need regular replacing.
- They may also shelter insect pests and small animals, such as field mice, gophers, and voles, which damage vine trunks and roots.

Organic herbicides such as herbicidal soaps or organic acids are formulated to damage any green vegetation, which includes vines. Apply these solutions as directed to the foliate of unwanted plants, taking care to avoid green grapevine tissue. Regular applications are essential, as these products do not remain active for long.

Pests and Diseases

Pest and disease management in vineyards is required all year. Be proactive rather than reactive. Thorough, comprehensive pest management allied with good cultural practices goes a long way to preventing and eradicating pests and diseases. Research the pests most likely to frequent your vineyard, together with management solutions. Invest in the correct application equipment where necessary.

Below are several common vineyard pests and diseases you'll need to know about if you are growing your own grapes (Cult Wine Investment, 2021):

- Roundworms or nematodes feed on vine roots. Planting resistant rootstocks is the only way to prevent roundworms from proliferating throughout your vineyard.
- Leafhoppers feed on wine leaves, leaving dead white spots. Eventually, affected leaves fall off, making the fruit susceptible to sunburn. Vines become less productive. Natural controls include:

  - spiders and parasitic mites
  - removing grass and weeds where leafhoppers congregate
  - spraying organic soaps and oils directly onto vines

- As mentioned previously, phylloxera is a microscopic aphid that feeds on grapevine roots. It still exists today in very old vineyards. North American rootstocks are resistant to it, so European varieties are grafted onto American rootstocks.

- Mealybugs live inside the wood of vine trunks to emerge in summer. They find the grapes and deposit scores of egg sacs and larvae, forcing wine growers to discard infected bunches. Ladybirds and wasps feed on the bugs, so winemakers encourage these beneficial insects in vineyards. Training vines so the grapes aren't touching the wood also helps.
- Powdery mildew is a fungus that covers both vines and fruit with a white powder. This prevents photosynthesis and compromises the grapes. Spores are borne on the wind or spread via raindrops, so the fungus spreads rapidly. It overwinters in dormant branches. It's almost impossible to eradicate, requiring careful vigilance and constant mitigation, especially with fungicides and sulfur dust.
- Another challenging fungal disease is downy mildew, which appears in the fall when temperatures drop. Symptoms include bright green patches, oil spots, and a moldy covering on the leaves that prevents photosynthesis. Powdery mildew attacks grape berries, so they shrivel and dry out. Take preventative steps, as there are no effective cures.
- Incurable Pierce's disease is spread by sap-feeding insects in Europe and California. This bacterial infection shuts down the water transport systems within the plant, so the vine eventually dies. Insecticides and biological controls like parasitic wasps that feed on the bugs are good preventatives.
- Also called gray mold or bunch rot, Botrytis fungus usually erupts during wet weather, although it can appear at any time. It initially discolors the grapes as it enters the berries, and they look blue and fuzzy. You will also notice a vinegary smell. Once it's taken hold, it is almost impossible

to eradicate, as it multiplies rapidly. Vineyards are experimenting with rain shelters to prevent its spread. White grape varieties can benefit from Botrytis, however, as affected grapes make wonderful desert wines. This is why Botrytis is sometimes called noble rot. In some vineyards, Botrytis is actually allowed or even encouraged to develop to create distinctive wines.

Integrated Pest Management (IPM)

There is a growing awareness that toxic fungicides and insecticides can be toxic or debilitating to the beneficial insects that keep detrimental pests and diseases in check. Integrated pest management (IPM) combines biological, cultural, and chemical control methods to combat pests and diseases. The idea is to take preventative action so that vines and grapes aren't damaged in the first place. IPM won't eradicate every single insect in the vineyard but controls detrimental insects so their activities cause minimal economic harm to the vineyard.

IPM involves (Goldammer, 2021):

- monitoring vines and grapes for pests
- correctly identifying pests
- accurately measuring vineyard pest populations
- developing standards for economic thresholds (the point where pests begin impacting the vineyard's economic viability)
- assessing damage levels
- implementing IPM tactics
- keeping records

Implementing IPM requires a thorough knowledge of common pests and their lifecycles, as well as the different strategies and products that could be used for pest control. Several control methods are often used simultaneously.

Control Methods Used in IPM

Cultural pest control disrupts the way pests interact with their hosts, so pests are less likely to grow, reproduce, and survive. High humidity and water buildup on vines promote diseases. Managing vines so they are drier creates conditions unfavorable for pests and diseases. Sloping ground and effective pruning promote airflow through the vineyard. Felling trees and removing structures that shade parts of the vineyard also help.

Biological control involves using beneficial insects and organisms that prey on pests. Bio-control agents include predatory wasps and mites, parasitic insects, and soil-dwelling mites. These won't wipe out the populations of troublesome insects, but they will keep them in check.

Biorational pesticides are grouped according to their shared characteristics, such as rapid degradation, requiring only small applications to be effective, and having ingredients that won't damage the natural environment. Many are approved for organic growing.

Biopesticides are derived from plants, bacteria, and minerals. Examples include:

- Biochemical pesticides use several methods to disrupt the lifecycles and movements of pests. For example, they may contain nature-identical, pheromone-like substances to prevent insects from mating, or scented plant extracts to draw insects into traps.
- Microbial pesticides have a fungus, bacterium, or protozoan as the active ingredient.

Conventional, synthetic pesticides and herbicides are the largest group of controls used by growers. These are mainly grouped into organochlorines, organophosphates, carbamates, and pyrethroids. If other IPM tactics are insufficient and the vineyard is likely to sustain significant economic losses, then these substances may be used after thoughtful research. If you do need to use these products, it's very helpful to understand how they work, as well as their human health impacts. You can learn more by consulting the work of the Insecticide Resistance Action Committee at https://irac-online.org/documents/moa-brochure.

Organic products are often rotated with chemical controls. Using bio-fungicides early in the season prevents diseases from taking hold while ensuring better plant health. They can be used throughout the growing season. Natural compounds in bioinsecticides repel insects, prevent them from feeding, reduce their reproduction, and eliminate them. For example, stylet oil is used to control many grapevine pests, such as leafhoppers, mites, scale, mealybugs, and leaf miners, and also prevents the spread of viruses transmitted by aphids.

ANNUAL CALENDAR OF VINEYARD MAINTENANCE

Use the following calendar as a quick reference guide as to what to do in your vineyard and when (Burrows, 2020). Be sure to adjust the months if you live in the southern hemisphere!

January–February

- Learn about wine grape production and network with growers at meetings.
- Build relationships with buyers.

- Develop a business plan for the year, including finances, goals and strategies, and work schedule.
- Review weed, insect, and disease management strategies.
- Review supplies and order where necessary.
- Check and repair equipment.

March–April

- Do soil tests and get an analysis done at a laboratory.
- Repair trellises and posts.
- Evaluate winter bud and cane damage.
- Remove old, diseased clusters remaining on vines.
- Get ready to receive new plants and prepare the lands.
- Eliminate and control weeds. (Do this before bud break.)
- Train vineyard personnel.
- Prune vines, checking for diseases and cane borer damage. Weigh the prunings for each vine.
- As per soil and petiole tests, add half the recommended nutrients to the soil.
- Check, prepare, and repair the irrigation system.
- Plant new, dormant vines.

May

- Monitor soil moisture and begin irrigating if required.
- Check for insects, especially those that may damage buds and new shoots.
- To control fungal diseases, add lime sulfur with dormant oil sprays as buds begin to develop. If buds burst before this, only add lime sulfur.
- Thin out shoots and clusters (late May).
- Control weeds around new plantings.
- Mow between grapevine rows.

June

- In early June, train new grape plantings onto trellises and remove any buds.
- Irrigate where needed—monitor new vines, as they will have shallow roots.
- Spray vines with fungicides, starting at 2 to 6 centimeters (1 to 3 inches) shoot growth until just before plants bloom. Thereafter, repeat according to product label recommendations for the next two to four weeks.
- Monitor insect pests and diseases and take action as needed.
- Weed around new plantings.
- Remove suckers from the bases of vines.
- Mow between grapevine rows.
- Toward the end of June, complete thinning out clusters and shoots, and position vigorous vines as needed, making sure leaves do not overlap.
- During blooming:
- Apply the second half of your recommended fertilizer program.
- Record the bloom time for each variety you are growing.

July

- Check your bird netting.
- Continue training new plantings.
- Continue with your pest control program.
- Complete positioning of the shoots.
- Apply pest management measures at pre-harvest recommendations.
- Mow between grapevine rows.
- Irrigate vines as needed.

- During veraison:
    - Remove leaves shading the fruit.
    - Collect leaf petioles for nutrient analysis.
    - If bunch rot was previously problematic, apply fungicides before installing netting.
    - Install bird netting as soon as the grapes start changing color. Remember to remove vine tendrils from the top of the trellis first.
    - Check the nets regularly for birds that might be caught in them.
- Preparing for the harvest:
    - Arrange additional labor.
    - Check supplies such as buckets, bins, pruners, etc.

August

- Contact and train harvest labor.
- Contact buyers and wineries to discuss the harvest.
- Check fruit for maturity, monitoring sugar levels, acidity, and flavor.
- Start harvesting early cultivars.
- Continue training new plantings and controlling weeds around the plants.
- Irrigate as needed but start reducing water quantities so vines can harden off.
- Mow between grapevine rows.
- Check for fungal diseases, especially anthracnose.

September

- Continue harvesting and checking for grape maturity.
- Continue disease management procedures.
- Plan new plantings. Plow and prepare new ground if necessary.
- Irrigate sparingly as needed.
- Clean all equipment.

October–November

- Remove any diseased fruit from the vineyard and dispose of it.
- Repair equipment.
- Order plants if you plan to plant more vines the following year.

Growing your own grapes is just one part of the winemaking process. You might be keen to turn your winemaking hobby into a small business. In the next chapter, you'll find out how to sell your wines commercially.

11

SELLING YOUR OWN WINE

> *No longer drink water exclusively, but use a little wine for the sake of your stomach and your frequent ailments.*
>
> — 1 TIMOTHY 5:23, THE BIBLE

> *Wine to me is passion. It's family and friends. It's warmth of heart and generosity of spirit. Wine is art. It's culture. It's the essence of civilization and the art of living.*
>
> — ROBERT MONDAVI

So you really want to get into winemaking and you'd like to earn extra income from your hobby? In this chapter, you'll find out how to sell your wine commercially.

Important note: As with Chapter 10, this chapter is intended for readers who would like to turn their winemaking hobby into a potential business. If you'd prefer to keep things small and simple, that's fine, too.

COMMERCIAL VERSUS HOMEMADE WINES

Before going commercial, it's important to understand the differences between commercial and homemade wines. Wine lovers might favor one over the other. There are four areas where commercial wines can be distinguished from homemade ones (Hansen, n.d.).

Taste

Commercial wines all taste pleasant, with pricier wines having better flavors and aromas. Homemade wines vary from undrinkable to fabulous. This is because professional winemakers have access to high-quality grapes grown to exacting standards. They have years of training and experience and better equipment. Nonprofessionals can also make wine with much better flavors and aromas than store-bought wines, so don't doubt yourself.

Chemical Compounds

Commercial wines often contain chemicals such as thickeners, color additives, sweeteners, and sulfites. Homemade wines don't contain these chemicals and are either sulfite-free or have much lower levels of sulfites. Imported wines might be stored in warehouses for a long time, so winemakers add more sulfites to ensure the integrity of the wine.

Price

Homemade wines are inexpensive to produce after purchasing the initial equipment, and the ingredients are not exorbitantly priced. Commercial wine prices fluctuate considerably depending on the brand, ingredients, country of origin, and production processes.

Because commercial winemakers produce wine at scale, these factors impact their prices.

Health Benefits

Red wine purportedly has several health benefits, which can be enhanced when wine is homemade. Organic winemakers can source grapes that have been grown without using harmful chemicals. Homemade wines contain fewer chemicals and are better for your health.

Benefits and Disadvantages of Homemade Wines

Advantages	Disadvantages
Cost-effective	Headaches are possible due to excessive tannins and histamines, especially when winemakers are new.
Easy to make	There is the possibility of contamination due to inadequate sterilization or chemicals leaching from containers.
Variety of flavors	
Hobby that could become a business	

Advantages and Disadvantages of Commercial Wines

Advantages	Disadvantages
Easy to obtain from retail stores	It might be difficult to find a wine you like.
Plenty of options to choose from	Commercial wines contain additional chemicals to preserve them.
Pricing is variable, so you can choose a wine to suit your budget	Some people are allergic to sulfites.

ALCOHOL REGULATIONS AND LICENSING

Producing and selling alcoholic beverages is highly regulated in most countries. You'll often need to comply with a suite of regulations, not to mention receiving special licenses.

You must navigate the red tape before you produce your first vintage so you have all the legal permissions, permits, and licenses in place. These depend on what you will be doing: Do you want to produce alcoholic beverages, sell them, or produce *and* sell alcoholic beverages? Who will you sell and ship them to—consumers, retailers, wholesalers, or all of these? Will you serve alcohol at your winery? How will you deliver it?

In the United States, for example, you'll need a federal license and an operating state license. Then, you'll need to register in the states where your customers reside, register your particular products (both federally and in applicable states), and register to collect and pay applicable taxes. You will need to take into account your country's legal definition of an alcoholic beverage, the legal drinking age (if you wish to serve wine on-site), and penalties for noncompliance.

If you wish to sell your wines online, you might also need to take note of personal privacy laws when collecting your customer's information. Make sure that your website and other materials adhere to these regulations and laws.

If you plan to offer food along with wine tastings at your winery, you may need to comply with public health regulations pertaining to restaurant facilities, for example.

Your labels and packaging might need to bear disclaimers according to local laws and regulations. In California, for example, liquor packaging needs to contain appropriate health warnings. If you are using plastic packaging, that might need to have health warnings, too.

In some cases, your logistics and transport suppliers might need to have special registrations to ship alcoholic beverages as well. Ensure that your shippers are compliant with all applicable laws.

Decide exactly how you plan to sell your wines and what kind of set-up you envisage having, like a winery with a tasting room and restaurant, and contact a lawyer who specializes in this field. That way, you can make sure of all laws that would apply to your business and ensure that you have all the right permits and permissions before you start.

BRANDING AND MARKETING STRATEGIES

To build a strong, successful brand, you need to answer a few questions at the outset (Wilson, 2022):

- What do you want your brand to achieve?
- Who are you trying to reach? Who is your target market?
- How do you want others to perceive you and your business?
- How is your brand different from your competitors?
- What do you want to tell your target market?
- How will your brand differentiate itself?
- Where and how will you promote your brand?
- How much money can you invest?
- When do you want to realize your goals? What is your timeline?

Hallmarks of a Successful Brand

It's worth taking a look at what makes a brand successful (Forbes Council Member, 2022).

- A daringly unique brand in a world of options stands out from the crowd. This may require some risk-taking but it creates brand loyalty.
- Brands with strong values have nothing to hide. When good values underpin a brand, its representatives make better decisions, brand messaging invokes these values, and their clients know who it is.
- Successful brands have an excellent understanding of their customers. Undertake in-depth research, so you know your target market, the challenges they face, the way they resolve them, who they follow, what their interests are, and where they socialize. This enables you to design your brand in such a way that your audience will find it irresistible.
- Consumers support brands that respond to them. Listen to your customers and give them what they are looking for.
- Brands with interesting stories generate more attention. Stories create trust and connectivity.
- Use superior content your customers can relate to. Think about how your content will connect you with your customers. Position your brand as a force to be reckoned with.
- Be clear about your mission and values. Define them, publish them, and communicate them effectively. This will give your target audience confidence in your brand.
- Be honest, memorable, and unforgettable. Your target audience will be more inclined to trust you.

- Obtain testimonials to show that you can deliver on your promises. People want to hear about others' experiences with your brand and wines. Focus on obtaining great testimonials to generate confidence in your wines.
- Know what your customers need. It's often the simple things that count. Work on building empathy and developing a reputation for thoughtfulness and attention to detail.
- Make sure you deliver. Your actions and the superiority of your product should back up your talk. Make sure your wines are as good as your brand marketing says they are.
- Find ways for your brand to make the world a better place because your wine is in it. People want to connect with brands and products that are doing good. Consider how you could work this into your mission and values.
- Merchandise can be useful. Think about things that you could give away with your wine—branded wine accessories, wine glasses, champagne buckets, and more.
- Ensure that all elements of your brand are aligned with one another. Your brand should be reinforced everywhere it appears, as this will make it successful.

Know Your Customers

It's essential that you identify your potential customers. Wine connoisseurs, collectors, millennials, or traditional wine consumers all look for different things, so ensure that your label appeals to the right target market.

Spend some time thinking about them. Consider their age, gender, income, marital status, careers, hobbies, and interests (which will tell you where and how they might consume your wines), whether they are environmentally conscious, and anything else that might make a potential consumer a good fit for your wines. Write these down.

CREATING A UNIQUE BRAND IDENTITY

Consumers use logos and labels to make purchasing decisions, so these are very important. They not only enable buyers to differentiate between brands and products, but they are also your silent ambassadors, endorsing your wine wherever it is. Customers will find out more about you and your wines and decide whether they would like to try drinking them.

Today's consumers are becoming more conscious, so your logo and labels can also confirm your wine's authenticity, organic origins, and artisanal roots.

Designing Your Logo

A logo identifies your business. It's another way to be distinctive. It's a unique symbol that appears on your labels, marketing material, website, and merchandise—everywhere your business is represented. However, it isn't your brand or even your visual identity.

There are different types of logos (Begg, 2023):

- Emblems are often used to identify wineries. These traditional logos combine an icon or symbol with text. These logos hint at formality and strength but may lose some of their detail when downscaled for printing.
- Logo symbols are icons (think Apple). While pictorial images bridge languages and cultures and are often effective and simple, it can be difficult to establish brand identity without text. Make sure your icon connects clearly with your brand.

- Wordmarks such as Google create a logo from the brand name. This works well if your business has a distinctive, catchy name.
- Monogram logos or lettermarks are similar, although they use acronyms. Examples are IBM and NASA. These logos are memorable and easy to scale up or down. As a new entrant into the market, you might need to state your business name below it.
- Abstract logos, such as the Pepsi logo, are distinctive pictorial representations of a brand. They use simple, bold shapes and colors. They can be obscure if your brand is not established in the market.
- Mascot logos use illustrated, cartoonish characters to convey a family-friendly, relaxed image. If you have a family-friendly brand, these logos are wonderful and they make it easy to build a brand story but they are unsuitable for more sophisticated brands. The artwork is complex and can be difficult to print.
- Combination logos combine both text and an icon. This is very versatile and enables your logo to have many variations. The brand message is clear due to the combination of image and text.

Use the following steps to design your logo (Begg, 2023):

1. Ensure that your logo is simple, original, and versatile. Consider something that would appeal to your target market.
2. Brainstorm words that describe your brand; use a thesaurus.
3. Sketch visual ideas based on these. Keep them simple and strategic. Don't use more than three colors. Choose one or two sketches you like and fine-tune them.

4. Show your ideas to people in your target market and obtain feedback.
5. Refine the most suitable sketch.
6. Develop your logo on a free design platform or work with a graphic designer to choose a font, pick versatile colors, and ensure scalability. Consider your brand's story when choosing colors and fonts. Avoid standard fonts. Find something different and exciting.

Designing Your Wine Label

Before starting your label design, ensure that you are familiar with your country's legislation. Your label should include all required elements on either the front or the back (or both).

Your wine label should include (Patterson, 2023):

- your brand name, prominently displayed
- type of wine, so your customers know whether they're buying a Cabernet Sauvignon or a Merlot (this will be determined by the color, fruit, and region)
- whether your wine has been blended with a foreign wine, together with the percentage
- the alcohol content per volume
- any health warning statements mandated by law
- the name and address of the bottler, usually preceded by "Produced and bottled by"
- how much wine is in the bottles in milliliters
- whether the wine contains sulfites, as some consumers are sensitive to sulfur
- country of origin, even if you produced the wine locally
- a fanciful name separate from the brand name or the wine type

Showcasing Your Brand

The shape of your wine bottle can be used as a marketing tool, and it's just as important as its quality. This means your bottles don't necessarily need to conform to the standard wine bottle designs referred to in Chapter 7. In fact, wineries often design unique bottle shapes for their high-end wines, and some are glass-blown works of art.

A study conducted in early 2003 found that the shoulders of wine bottles appealed to consumers, followed by the tops, centers, and finally the bottoms (Ozturk et al., 2003). Bottles with shorter shoulders and sharply cut lines got more attention than bottles with sloping shoulders. The study concluded that logos should be placed on the shoulders of the bottles to have the greatest chance of being read by consumers.

People are naturally drawn to labels—make sure they're yours. Your labels need to be eye-catching and unique. You will be competing with numerous winemakers and cellars, so they need to be outstanding. Consider how you could create a striking label to differentiate your wine from others. If you want to build your brand, people need to instantly see and identify your wines, so consider what elements of the label design are brand-related, and which ones can be varied depending on factors such as the blend or vintage.

Before designing your labels, visit a few wine shops or look at online stores to see what other wine producers are doing. People are creatures of habit, so you might be able to adapt the strategies used by big cellars and well-known brands.

Think about what you want to tell your potential customers about your wine. Is it elegant, sophisticated, traditional, fun, or just fabulous wine? Wine labels can connect with history and culture.

Artwork may incorporate abstract or contemporary designs, simplicity, humor, or drama.

As mentioned previously, wine bottle colors may be dark or light green, clear, or amber. Your label colors can either complement the bottles or contrast with them. If you have some extra printing budget, consider foil stamping. This glints in the light, highlighting your bottles. Choose a typeface that suits your label and wine type. Bold typography is essential. Don't use more than three fonts, as this can make the label look crowded and disjointed (Patterson, 2023). Check online for the latest fonts to give you a starting point.

There are several materials you can use for your labels. Heavy, textured paper, embossed letters, die-cutting, and metallic polypropylene are all options. Embossing and stamping may give your wine a luxurious, sophisticated feel or you can add some texture. Die-cutting creates numerous shapes, so you aren't limited to standard or rectangular labels.

Plastic labels are a good choice for wines served chilled. Having some transparency means the wine can speak for itself. Alternatively, opt for a metallic label. Both choices will complement and enhance your graphic design. Unlaminated paper labels provide texture. However, they are water-resistant, not waterproof, so could be compromised if the bottle is damp or wet. They could be a good choice for wines served at room temperature.

Don't forget about the boxes the wine will be packaged in. Ensure that the designs complement the labels—and remember to add your logo to your labels and boxes.

Hiding in Plain Sight: Good Wines With Bad Labels

Clever, contemporary labels will often have consumers reaching for the bottle, even though good labeling doesn't necessarily mean that there's a quality wine inside. This means that the label design is effective.

All art, including a label, is subjectively interpreted by those who see it. Generic labels featuring flowers, vehicles, or cute animals are frequently used for cheap, mass-produced wines. However, this is not always the case. Zinfandels high in alcohol sometimes bear labels more appropriate for energy drinks—but the wine is fabulous.

Many top wines still bear traditional, understated labels featuring chateaux, crests, shields, or landscapes. Some cellars even get famous artists to design their labels. Labels should ideally reflect the contents of the bottle, but this doesn't always happen. Some superb wines have labels featuring goth masks, blindfolded prisoners, and monster wars. All these wines are pricey and they taste incredible.

Tips for Wine Labels

- Labels must be easily readable. Avoid things like fuzzy white type on a dark background.
- All technical information must be accurate, telling consumers more about your wine.
- Avoid spelling errors, poor color choices, generic text, and fonts that create unclear text.
- Some of your information might need to be approved by an industry body or government department. Check before writing up your labels and ensure that you have the right approvals.
- The alcohol percentage stated on the label should be legible, as it helps consumers make informed choices.

- Use regional appellations wherever possible. In the United States, state your American Viticultural Area (AVA) on your label.
- Mention which grapes were used and where you sourced them from. Wine drinkers love this.
- If you have green certification, ensure that these logos are also displayed on the bottles, together with a link to your website or that of the certification body so customers can obtain more information about it.
- Avoid generic, often meaningless terms such as bold, dream, passion, finest, handcrafted, noble, reserve, and world-class.

Writing Your Brand Story

This tells your customers about your business's mission and builds their trust. It is emotive and even compelling. It should be customer-focused, authentic, and consistent across all your narratives and marketing channels. Structure it like a story, with a simple, clear message and some vivid details. People like to connect through stories.

A brand story begins by identifying a problem the customer has. They then discover how your brand shares their values and solves their difficulty. Because you have connected with their emotional and physical needs, they are motivated to take action. This increases your visibility, sales conversions, and profitability.

Brand stories form part of your brand's identity and enable you to humanize your business. Many businesses focus on their inception but you can select any aspect of your business. The story communicates something about who you are and should include your brand's values and ideals. Having a brand story makes people feel they know you. Your brand becomes personal, so they trust you. Your story will also foster brand loyalty.

To create your brand story you need to (Romano, 2022):

- decide what message you want to convey.
- explain why you do it.
- tell your customers who you are.
- understand your target audience and create a story that resonates with them.
- build your narrative, explaining why you started your business, your vision, and how your brand works toward it, as well as what your brand plans for the future.
- find the right platforms to broadcast it.

Your brand story should (Romano, 2022):

- introduce your brand, explaining what it does and how it's unique.
- provide some background, such as why you began producing wine, as well as something about your inspiration and any challenges you have faced.
- explain the purpose of your brand, including its vision, mission, and values, as well as how your business aims to make a difference.
- explain how your brand is unique.
- describe your brand's personality.
- explain the customer experience your brand offers, such as how you meet their needs, how you solve their problems, and any support you provide.
- share some success stories.
- conclude by restarting your brand's purpose and unique value.

MARKETING YOUR WINE

There are several ways to market your wine. Adopt a suite of marketing options rather than focusing on a single avenue to give you a wider spread of opportunities to introduce your wine to potential customers.

The best way to market your wine is to let it speak for itself, especially if you're new in the market. Establish the special characteristics of your wines and find ways to introduce these to others. If you're just starting, people need to taste your wines.

You'll need a website, which can double as an e-commerce site and a social media presence. There are several ways to introduce your wines to others. Not everything you try will work, but over time, you'll establish what works best and focus on those avenues.

Wine Marketing Tips and Tricks

- Always showcase what makes your winery special and distinctive. Make people curious.
- Focus on your website, ensuring that it encapsulates the values and mission of your brand and showcases everything you offer. Include a wine list, a wine blog, and e-commerce options.
- Social media pages are a low-cost marketing option. Post about events and functions your winery has hosted, wine tastings, special menus, fun days—and your wines, of course.
- Use live videos to do virtual wine tastings, discuss wine pairings, and showcase anything wine-related.
- Develop a mailing list of potential and actual customers. Then, create a newsletter to send to them regularly. Keep it

interesting and topical. Share information about the grapes you use in your wines.

- Create wine-tasting kits, including a bottle or two of your wine, glasses, some wine accessories, and wine-tasting instructions.
- Sustainability is generating more interest, so incorporate sustainability into your operations and publicize what you are doing through your website and social media channels.
- Have a vintage sale of special wines.
- Invite local artists to a wine and painting evening at your winery.
- Raffle a bottle of wine at a local fete or on your website, if this is allowed in your country.
- Display your bottle labels on the walls of your winery. Over time, you'll have some great works of art that visitors might find interesting.
- Find a wine influencer to work with to promote your wines.
- Start a wine club. This is a great way to target wine lovers and you can work with other wineries to increase your offerings. Alternatively, get your wine listed with local and regional wine clubs.
- Offer free sample wine tastings. This is a great way to promote your wines to the public.
- Work with other local businesses to do joint promotions, special offers, and events. You'll become part of the local business community, and others might promote what you are doing. Create a map of local attractions so everyone can benefit from visitors.
- Sell your wine at farmer's markets, food fairs, beer festivals, music festivals, and similar outlets. Arrange pop-up wine tastings at these events.

- Create sub-brands to appeal to additional target markets, such as millennials.
- Stay customer-focused and remember that quality always comes to the fore!
- Track your results so you can identify which strategies are working. Marketing is hard work, so focus on things that generate interest and sales.

EXPORTING YOUR WINES

Once you've become established, you might want to export your wines. The wine market is booming: In 2022, over 1.9 billion bottles were shipped to more than 200 countries. The biggest wine importers were the United States, China, and Japan, with demand for sparkling and rosé wines increasing rapidly (Gori, 2023).

You'll need to do your research to establish whether there is a market for your wines overseas. Wine demand varies between countries and certain types of wine may not be as popular overseas as they are at home. Consider wine prices in your destination country and whether your prices would be competitive after taking into account shipping and other costs. For shipping, you can use air freight, ocean freight, or road transport. Each has benefits and drawbacks, so you need to decide which method would work best.

Research legislation and restrictions that might apply in your home country. Some places have restrictions on the volume or value of wine that can be exported, for example. Determine which rules apply to your situation. You'll also need to find out about import, export, and quality regulations, as well as taxes and customs duties at the destination port.

Find out what trade agreements exist between your country and your intended destinations. These set down what items can be shipped, as well as the taxes and duties that apply. Even if your country has no restrictions on alcoholic exports, your destination countries might, so get all the information beforehand. There may be specific requirements for different types of wine. Check on all these before exporting.

Once you have cleared the legal hurdles, you might choose to use a freight forwarder to handle the shipment for you. These services take care of everything, from negotiating prices to arranging insurance and customs payments. Regulatory details can be extensive, so using a freight handler might help you negotiate the red tape.

ONLINE PLATFORMS FOR SMALL QUANTITIES

If you are selling only relatively small quantities of wine, the websites listed below can help you sell online.

- Wine Searcher: https://www.wine-searcher.com
- Cellar Bid: https://www.cellarbid.com/html/sellers_guide.htm
- Wine Industry: https://wineindustry.com
- Vivino: https://www.vivino.com/US/en
- Drizly: https://drizly.com
- CellarLink: https://www.cellarlink.com.au/buy-wine-online/store/storeclosed
- Bid for Wine: https://www.bidforwine.co.uk
- Sell Your Wine https://cultwinesintl.com/sell-us-your-wine

Part of what makes winemaking such an absorbing and rewarding hobby is that you'll never stop learning and growing as a person and a winemaker. In the next chapter, you'll discover the fulfillment that comes from being part of a winemaking community, as well as how to improve your skills and pass your knowledge on to others.

12

THE JOURNEY CONTINUES

> *Wine improves with age. The older I get, the better I like it.*
>
> — ANONYMOUS

> *A meal without wine is like a day without sunshine.*
>
> — JEAN ANTHELME BRILLAT-SAVARIN

Once you start making your own wines, you'll discover that this isn't just a once-off event but a lifelong passion. Becoming part of the winemaking community will continue to inspire you as you share your enthusiasm with like-minded people. You might also want to pass on your knowledge. In this chapter, you'll discover how to achieve these goals.

JOINING A WINE COMMUNITY

Winemakers cross the world are joining forces to improve the quality and visibility of their wines and promote one another's efforts. Different winemaking groups have diverse goals but the emphasis is on collaboration. Most groups offer a platform for winemakers to discuss common issues.

- Situated in Burgenland, Austria, Pannobile offers opportunities for local winemakers to create new wines and blends. Despite having many different winemaking styles, winemakers collaborate to develop superior wines known as Pannobile wines. The standards are high and tasting decisions must be unanimous. The group gets together in January to taste everyone's individual vintages.
- Club Trésors de Champagne in Reims, France, showcases only the best of their members' wines. Most members are small-scale operators who promote one another's wines and educate people about champagne. Members compete for the group's "Special Club" award—wines that receive the label are aged for three years and shipped to retailers worldwide. The club has its own store in Reims. Tastings and education are a feature of the store and members take turns to work there.
- New Mission Winemakers is located in San Francisco. Founded by two former winemakers, the club offers opportunities for local winemakers to show off their wines to the public and other producers. The concept includes post-harvest tastings and other events. The idea is to promote new winemakers whose wines are not well-known.
- Zoo Cru in South Africa's Western Cape evolved out of newcomers' inability to make a splash at Cape Town's

biggest wine trade show. A small group of winemakers built a contemporary stand that attracted a significant amount of attention. The winemakers don't use the term outside of the shows and focus on producing their own vintages. The group has grown and the idea is to keep things interesting with different members running the stand in different years.

- Cercle Ruster Ausbruch is located near the Austrian town of Rust and was originally formed to bolster the sweet wine industry's tarnished image after some producers encountered negative publicity. The club's focus is Ruster Ausbruch, a premium Botrytized wine. The group initially focused on creating a distinctive sweet wine and held regular tastings to approve members' wines. Today, they focus on marketing and successful collaborations. They hope to have Ruster Ausbruch formally recognized as a premium wine.

Finding Winemaker Communities: Resources

As an aspiring home winemaker, you will be well served to connect with local amateur winemakers who have valuable experience and understanding of the local terroir. A good example in my hometown of Lodi, California is the Lodi Amateur Vintners Association, or LAVA, which has monthly meetings, guest speakers, and resources for the membership and the general public.

The Wine International Association offers a B2B network for the wine industry, focusing on the commercial aspects. The organization arranges global expos, showcases the vineyards of its members, and offers promotional and marketing opportunities in 180 countries. For more information, visit

https://wineinternationalassociation.org.

WineMaker magazine has a directory of both formal and informal winemakers' clubs and associations across the United States, including ones geared toward home winemakers. For more information, visit

https://winemakermag.com/resource/club-directory.

For information on winemakers guilds and associations worldwide for both professionals and amateurs, visit

https://amateurwine.org.au/web-links#winemakers-guilds.

Geared to amateur winemakers, the Winemakers Club in London, United Kingdom, showcases wines from small producers, selling them at its shop and online There are regular wine tastings and a bar on-site. Email them at

shop@thewinemakersclub.co.uk.

HOW WINEMAKING CHANGES YOU

The world of wine is an intriguing one. Even as a relative outsider, there are stories of people who grew up in winemaking families—the dynasties that have been making wine for generations and passing down their techniques. Many winemakers don't have any winemaking background and might have happened on it as a second or third career after someone gifted them with a winemaking kit or they started a new hobby. Many started with no financial backing and little money—and I have yet to meet one with any regrets.

Erich was going to be a cardiologist but switched to English literature. After a career of fits and starts—he worked as a health insurance salesman, male model, and waiter—he discovered that he enjoyed service and sales. The restaurant where he waited tables promoted him to wine buyer. He began writing a wine blog and was hooked. In 2004, Erich left his hometown of Chicago and headed to the Pacific Northwest, where he worked his first wine harvest in the Willamette Valley. He was then offered an opportunity to teach English. He loved it but burnt out after six years. A friend who worked in the vineyards offered him an opportunity to work another harvest. This time, the winemaking bug bit, and he's been making his own wine ever since, developing his brand and loving it.

Emily worked as a medical researcher after getting a biotech degree, but she spent her evenings working as a taster for a Seattle winery. She loved wine and wondered whether her science background might open a door. Encouraged by a friend, she worked as a harvest intern at a Washington winery. By the end of the season, she was working there permanently as a lab tech. She moved between wineries and is now head winemaker for a Californian winery. She's also working on a project where the winery's fruits and vegetables will be donated to local food banks.

Kat began her career working with children in crisis at foster care centers. Emotionally drained after several years, she embarked on a global backpacking tour. A year later, she found herself almost broke in New Zealand and took a harvest job at a winery. She worked in the cellar and loved every minute. She's still working in the New Zealand wine industry, where she's an assistant winemaker in Marlborough.

PUSHING THE BOUNDARIES

When making wine, it's entirely appropriate to do a little experimenting. Making bold choices is a good way to learn about wine and the winemaking process. Here are some alternatives to try (*Experimenting With Wine*, 2019):

- Instead of Cabernet Sauvignon, drink Nero d'Avola, a light red Sicilian wine. The Cabernet Sauvignon is blended with other grapes and has chalky tannin flavors. Another alternative is Touriga Nacional from Portugal. These grapes are normally used to make port but the wine has a distinctive taste and aroma.
- Sauvignon Blanc can be replaced with Vermentino from Italy, a refreshing, slightly bitter-tasting wine with pear and citrussy pink notes. Another alternative is Falanghina, also from Italy. This is one of the world's oldest grape varieties and produces a light wine.

- Chardonnay is popular, especially on hot summer days. Try a quality dry Riesling instead. You'll also get those crisp, dry flavors and intense aromas with Albarino from Spain.
- Syrah or Shiraz is a firm international favorite. Grenache has largely been forgotten but makes a wonderfully bold red wine. Barolo is considered one of Italy's best wines, and is well worth drinking, while Malbec is a gentle, fruity French wine.

Wine Industry Innovations

Welcome to an industry that is the essence of creativity! From times immemorial, farmers have adapted their practices to respond to prevailing challenges. This is true more than ever today. Keep an eye out for research yielding innovative solutions to age-old problems. An Oregon winery has built a UV robot to counteract powdery mildew, while Burgundy winemakers are tackling extreme weather by shooting silver iodine particles into the air to generate a protective hail shield. As a taste for wine-drinking spreads to new parts of the globe, expect groundbreaking technologies to revolutionize the way growers do business.

Wineries are using new technologies to improve wine production in the following ways:

- Optical sorters are making it easier to separate the good from the bad, as they can be programmed to discard stems, rotten grapes, and debris.
- New technologies allow winemakers to watch and assess the behavior of sediments in bottles. This can inform them about operational issues such as the best bottle shapes to

use, the development of the wine in the bottle, and other aspects of winemaking.

- Maceration accelerators section grape skins so a larger portion of the surface area is in contact with the must. This increases the extraction of certain compounds and reduces production time.
- Advanced cooling systems enable winemakers to better control storage temperatures. Wines are more stable and have better color.
- Aluminum closures used at contemporary wineries can verify the purchaser's location, information that can be used for marketing and logistics.

There are now novel ways of aging wines. One winery sent over 300 of its Petrus vintage and vine canes into orbit. When they returned, the vines grew faster than Earth-bound ones, and the wine also aged more quickly. Some winemakers are working on underwater aging, which provides the equivalent of a year of aging in just one month (Cult Wine Investment, 2021).

Technology is also innovating packaging. One winery's label tells its brand story with a multimedia presentation when scanned with the buyer's phone. Another packaging trend are single-serve wine bottles, cans, or aluminum wine bottles. This is fast becoming a global industry. Boxed wines are considered more portable, convenient, and safe than glass bottles.

In our quick-dry paint world, if you don't want to wait half an hour for your wine to chill in the refrigerator, you can use Juno. This device uses reverse microwave technology to chill wine super fast. Your bottle will reach the right temperature in just three minutes (Cult Wine Investment, 2021).

Wine tasting can be fun and blind tastings tell winemakers a great deal about their wines so they can make improvements. Now artificial intelligence analyzes thousands of wines a year, producing data winemakers can use to determine the best tanks to use when blending.

Blended vintages are becoming more acceptable, with many consumers looking for easy-drinking wines that taste good. Wine brands are becoming similar to supermarket wines with fun, innovative labeling. Wine retail is changing, with sales becoming more experience-based, including wine tastings and activities.

Repetitive, demanding vineyard tasks fall to workers who can be used more productively elsewhere. Wineries are using robots to do repetitive manual work such as weeding and mowing.

Counterfeiting wines is a massive risk for collectors, but blockchain and digital innovation are making this more difficult. Prooftag is a digital labeling system that uses digital ledgers to guarantee authenticity. The system is tamper-proof.

While screwcap bottles are being used to counter the very real problem of cork taint, NASA has developed tech based on analytical chemistry that could resolve the problem for good.

MASTERING THE ART OF WINEMAKING

If you've enjoyed making wine at home, you might want to become a professional winemaker, also known as an enologist or vintner. Besides growing grapes and making wine, winemakers build communities of wine enthusiasts and promote wines. They manage vineyards and production, oversee grape quality and fermentation, develop new wines, assist with packaging and distribution, track expenditures and income, supervise equipment and staff, ensure legal compliance, and keep meticulous records.

To become a professional winemaker, you will need (Indeed Editorial Team, 2022):

- a bachelor's degree majoring in viticulture, enology, horticulture, food science, or wine science
- additional courses in chemistry, biology, agriculture, marketing, and public relations
- experience in the wine industry, which you can gain by becoming an apprentice or an intern, or getting an entry-level or seasonal job

You can gain related experience by:

- joining wine-tasting groups
- working in a wine cellar
- writing articles and blogs about wine
- becoming a sommelier
- creating wine pairings for bars and restaurants
- selling seeds to vineyards or equipment to wineries
- working in a brewery or on a fruit farm

Winemaking is collaborative, so build networks by going to tastings and joining clubs, attending trade shows, industry conventions, and events, connecting with wineries that supply restaurants, and meeting suppliers, vendors, and potential customers. General business and marketing skills will also be beneficial.

OTHER WINE INDUSTRY CAREERS

Sommelier

Sommeliers are wine stewards—trained, knowledgeable wine professionals who work in restaurants or the hospitality industry. They know which wines are available and can help consumers find wines of their choice.

Wine sommeliers (*How to Become a Wine Sommelier,* 2019):

- develop a restaurant or facility's wine list and wine program
- manage the wine inventory
- work with the chefs to determine food and wine pairings
- train staff about wine
- speak directly with patrons to make recommendations and answer questions
- know all the beverages served by the establishment

To become a sommelier, you'll need credentials. Some acclaimed accreditation schools include (*How to Become a Wine Sommelier,* 2019):

- Wine and Spirit Education Trust (United Kingdom)
- The Court of Master Sommeliers (United Kingdom)
- North American Sommelier Association (Canada and United States)
- Associazione Italiana Sommelier (Italy)

Wine Connoisseur

This is someone who has acquired extensive wine knowledge, from wine styles to aging and flavor profiles. Many have formal training and some are certified. To become a wine connoisseur, you will need to (Zhang, n.d.):

- understand the five S's of wine drinking—see, swirl, smell, sip, and savor
- have a robust working knowledge of terroir
- understand basic wine characteristics
- know different grape varieties and add to your knowledge as new cultivars are developed
- master wine description vocabulary
- be aware of which glass to use for different wines
- know the perfect serving temperatures
- attend wine-tasting events and organize tastings
- explore local wineshops
- create your own group of wine lovers
- understand different wine styles
- keep reading and learning
- get official certifications and credentials

Wine Expert

Becoming a wine expert can be daunting. If you're committed to the task, you could be a wine expert within a year. From there, you can move on to become a sommelier or connoisseur. Here are some quick guidelines for becoming a wine expert (Puckette, 2023):

- Develop your wine palate. Start slowly and follow the five S's outlined above. Taste a range of different wines—this might be easier if you join a wine-tasting group.
- Try new, distinctive wines, preferably from another wine region or even another part of the world.
- Read books about different vintages, wine guides, and wine encyclopedias.
- Drink bold wines such as Syrah or Shiraz Malbec, Petite Syrah, Mourvèdre or Monastrell, Touriga Nacional, Cabernet Sauvignon, or Petit Verdot.
- Expand your palate by drinking unusual and complex wines, as well as subtle, elegant wines.
- Discover Champagne and sweet wines.

By the time you've done all this, you should recognize wine by varietal and region and be able to pair food and wine. You'll feel confident when faced with a wine list. You'll have made friends with loads of other wine lovers.

PASSING IT ON: TEACHING OTHERS ABOUT WINEMAKING

If you love wine and have been making your own, you might want to become an educator in the field. Start slowly so you can see if this would suit you. Teach others informally through avenues like home wine tastings. Ask those who attended what they enjoyed about your presentation and where you might improve.

Get permission to train others at work, not necessarily about wine, but simply to get experience. Develop training session plans, ask for feedback, and learn how to build one-on-one relationships by serving others.

Put together a one-night wine appreciation course or a consumer wine course. Plan every aspect of the session and allow enough time for tasting different wines. Teach it to friends and family first to iron out any potential problems. Then, propose the course to an adult education center. Think about teachers whose approach you enjoyed and emulate them. Ask for feedback and continue improving your approach.

When you're ready, get in touch with a wine certification program and ask whether you can help run a course or teach their students. Find out as much as you can about the students and classroom and review the session plan beforehand. After the class, ask for feedback from your colleagues.

If you want to formally move into wine education, you must have good communication skills. This is probably more important than knowledge about wine, although that is advantageous, too. Obtain accreditation from an organization such as the Court of Master Sommeliers, the French Wine Scholar, or the Wine and Spirits Education Trust. This will give you access to syllabuses, course materials, administrative support, and other resources. You'll also become part of a global community!

You'll be teaching adults, so listen to your students, teach without being condescending, be inclusive, and always stay humble. Students working in the wine industry might find your courses helpful, but it's important to steer everyone in the right direction, regardless of their interests.

Besides teaching, you'll need to plan your lessons, develop session plans, research your lectures, and design classroom exercises. Expect to spend three hours in preparation for every hour in the classroom (*How to Become a Wine Educator*, 2021). There will be staff meetings to attend, and you'll need to allow time to communicate directly with students. You might also need to coordinate materials and wines for blind tastings.

Teaching about wine is a physical job, as you'll need to carry cases of wine, set up wine tastings, and clean up afterward. You might opt to teach part time, which many do, besides holding down a full-time job or enjoying other activities. You can use digital media to reach a wider audience with your classes.

Winemaking is an endless journey that will continuously offer you new and different experiences. Reflect on your own winemaking adventures as you continue growing in your winemaking endeavors.

RAISE A GLASS TO INSPIRE NEW WINEMAKERS!

You're at the start of a rewarding journey with endless possibilities. Why not take a moment to inspire someone else to follow the same road?

Simply by sharing your honest opinion of this book and a little about your experience with making wine, you'll inspire new readers to have a go themselves.

Thank you so much for your support. I raise my glass to you!

Scan the QR code for a quick review!

CONCLUSION

> *Wine is constant proof that God loves us and loves to see us happy.*
>
> — BENJAMIN FRANKLIN

> *Penicillin cures, but wine makes people happy.*
>
> — ALEXANDER FLEMING

Wine has been made since the time of the ancient Egyptians and Chinese. The Phoenicians brought wine to the Greeks, who in turn introduced it to the Romans. They spread wine culture through their Empire. During the Middle Ages, the churches continued producing wine for Holy Communion. The French aristocracy kept winemaking traditions alive, while historic explorers took European wines to the New World. The deadly phylloxera almost wiped out the global wine industry in the mid-1800s, but North American rootstocks that were resistant to the pest saved the day.

Today, the world's top grape-growing and wine-producing regions include several Western European countries, together with Australia, South Africa, and the United States. Wines are influenced by climatic factors, soils, and microflora, which taken together are known as the terroir of the wine.

To make wine, you'll need a fermentation vessel—either oak barrels, wooden tanks, stainless steel tanks, glass carboys, or large buckets. All have pros and cons. Stainless steel tanks are preferred for large quantities, while small-scale winemakers may use glass carboys or large plastic buckets. A range of smaller specialized equipment is required, together with regular kitchen utensils, yeast, and certain chemicals. Winemaking is relatively inexpensive after the initial outlay. Quality grapes can be sourced from several places and wine can also be made from other fruits.

Grapes are picked at different stages of ripeness, depending on the wine to be produced and how much sugar content is required. Grapes are sorted to remove stems, rotten grapes, and debris. Home winemakers do this by hand, while commercial wineries use special equipment. Grapes can be crushed mechanically or by foot treading. Afterward, the grapes are pressed to release the juice. When making red wine, the grape skins are left in the juice, as this gives the wine its color and tannins. They are strained out when white wine is produced. Whites are usually consumed young, while red wine can be aged for years.

Winemakers sometimes make errors, especially when they are beginners. It's important to be patient, have the right equipment, ensure that all your equipment and utensils are clean and properly sanitized, and that best practice methods are followed. There are steps you can take to retrieve your wine if things go wrong.

Fermentation takes place in a fermentation vessel or tank. While the skins of grapes harbor natural yeasts, these are not always sufficient or desirable. Winemakers add specially formulated commercial yeasts to ensure effective fermentation. Yeast turns the natural sugars in the grape juice into alcohol to make wine. When selecting a yeast strain, check its requirements for temperature, alcohol tolerance, foam production, flocculation, fermentation rate, and the production of volatile acids, sulfur dioxide, and esters.

Fermentation temperatures need to be controlled to ensure desirable results. It's important to regulate the pH and prevent oxidation. Additional sulfur dioxide is added to preserve the wine when fermentation is completed. Wines should be stabilized and either filtered and bottled or aged.

Primary fermentation is of relatively short duration and requires oxygen to enter the mixture to facilitate the reaction. Secondary fermentation is a quieter process. Malolactic fermentation either begins simultaneously or is induced by the winemaker. This lowers the acidity of the wines and mellows them out. Oxygen should not enter fermenters during secondary fermentation or the wine may spoil.

Wines are often blended to balance out characteristics such as sweetness, acidity, tannins, alcohol levels, and body. Blending creates complex flavor profiles. It won't rescue a bad wine but it will rectify minor wine faults. Wine blending involves careful wine selection and tasting.

Wine is normally bottled in dark green or amber bottles to protect it from light. White and rose wines are bottled in clear glass bottles to showcase their natural colors. Packaging options such as boxes are used to protect these wines from light. There are different kinds of bottle closures, including natural corks, synthetic corks, and screwcaps. Ensure that bottled wines are stored correctly at the right temperatures so they don't deteriorate before you drink them.

Winemakers may encounter certain difficulties when making wine, especially when they are still gaining experience. Stuck fermentations have several causes, most often related to the yeast being used. Once these are resolved, the fermentation can continue. Unusual wine colors have different causes, some of which are resolvable, while others are not. Off-aromas can indicate several problems. Cork taint as a result of compromised corks also occurs.

Wine tasting is a great way to share and enjoy wine—and to introduce your wine to others. You can do tastings through wine clubs or wineries. To showcase your wines, arrange wine tasting at home. Wine is great when enjoyed with certain foods. When pairing is done correctly, it enhances the flavors of both the food and the wine. You can give your wine away as a gift for a wedding, special birthday, or other occasion.

If you want to have more control over your winemaking and the grapes you use, you could grow your own grapes. Ensure that your area has the right climate to grow grapes and cultivate vintages that thrive in your region. Choose a vineyard site that is slightly sloping, at the right elevation, and is not subject to excessive wind, frost, or humidity. Take soil samples and have them analyzed to determine your soil's nutritional status, pH, and other factors. Add nutrients as required before planting, as it's difficult to do this later. Construct trellises on the land—the type of trellis used will depend on which cultivars you are growing.

Once your grapes are planted, you will need to irrigate your vines during dry seasons or in between rainfall events. Withholding water at certain times in the growth cycle can be beneficial but don't overdo it. Take petiole samples and send them to a laboratory for analysis at least once a year to determine your vines' nutritional requirements. Add nutrients only if the analysis indicates that this is necessary. Keep an eye on your soil's pH, as this may affect nutrient availability for plants. Manage weeds and use integrated pest management (IPM) to control pests and diseases while keeping the use of harmful, toxic chemicals to a minimum.

If you wish to sell your wines commercially, make sure that you are compliant with the relevant laws in your country and that you have all the correct permits and licenses before you begin. Develop a strong brand by deciding on your mission, vision, and values. Then, create a logo reflecting these and tell your brand story. Develop wine labels that are legally compliant but striking and distinctive. There are numerous ways you can market your wines, from hosting wine-tasting events to using social media to build a following.

You may want to export your wines. Do thorough research into all aspects to ensure that you are compliant and familiar with all regulations, customs information, and costs, both in your own country and the destination countries. There are online platforms where you can sell small quantities of your wine.

Making your own wine is a continuous learning process. Join a winemaking community to mix with like-minded people, sharing hints and tips. Find wines that can be good substitutes for known wine types. Become conversant with new technologies that are making wine production easier and cheaper. You might want to embark on a formal career as a professional winemaker, sommelier, or connoisseur or simply become a wine expert.

Winemaking is a fascinating endeavor. It is my hope that you will take what you have learned in this book about the art and science of winemaking and put it into practice. The vineyard of knowledge is vast, and the best way to reap its fruits is to get your hands dirty and start your winemaking journey. Like life, wine is a continuous journey of growth, experience, friendships, flavors, and food.

GLOSSARY

Acidity: The sharpness or tartness of wine.

Aroma: The smell of wine, usually used to refer to younger wines.

Astringent: Caused by high tannin levels, this tasting term refers to the bitter taste and dryness in the mouth.

Balance: This is when the different components of the wine come together harmoniously.

Bold: Dark red wine, high in alcohol, with an intense flavor.

Bouquet: Complex aromas of aged wine.

Chaptalization: Adding sugar to unfermented grape juice so the alcohol level is increased. This is illegal or regulated in some countries.

Corking: The process of sealing wine bottles with corks.

Cooperage: Wine barrel maker.

Complex: Several scents or aromas are present in the wine; this usually indicates a superior quality wine.

Creamy: Wine with a texture similar to that of cream.

Crisp: This term refers to fruit that is crisp and acidic

Cru: French term referring to a particular place where wine is produced or a vineyard.

Crush: Harvest time. This is also when wine fermentation is done.

Decant: Pouring wine from a bottle into another container—usually a decanter. This aerates the wine and allows any sediment to separate.

Delicate: Light wines, usually white wines.

Destemming: Removal of grapes from the stems.

Dry: A sourish taste that makes the mouth pucker and is usually attributed to tannin levels in the wine.

Earthy: A flavor or aroma similar to moist soil.

Enologist: Winemaker.

Fermentation Lock: Device that allows fermentation gases to escape while sealing fermentation vessels.

Full-Bodied: Wine high in alcohol and flavor.

Fruity: A wine-tasting term that refers to wines that have an aroma and flavor reminiscent to that of fresh fruit.

Herbaceous: A tasting term referring to wine aromas and tastes similar to those of herbs like rosemary, basil, oregano, etc.

Hydrometer: Instrument used to measure the density of liquids.

Intensity: This usually happens when the wine is very flavorful.

Lees: Sediment at the bottom of the fermentation vessel.

Maceration: This is when wines are oxidized. The wines show aged colors and are not fruity.

Malolactic: Secondary fermentation that changes the tartness of malic acid into a smooth, creamy sensation.

Minerality: When vines are grown in rocky soils high in minerals, the resulting wine has the aroma and sensation of crushed rock or stone.

Must: Unfermented grape juice, which includes the skins, stems, and seeds.

Nutty: Usually refers to oxidized wines but can be used for sweet wines where the grapes were subject to Botrytis.

Oxidation: Exposing wines to air; this can spoil the wine.

Peppery: Wine that smells of white or black pepper.

Pomace: Seeds, skins, and stems that remain after the liquid is poured out of the vat. This is usually used to produce pressed wine, which has more tannins, color, and flavors. Pomace is sometimes added to the wine.

Racking: When wine is moved to another barrel to reduce sediment and add air to the wine.

Racking Cane: Tool used to siphon wine between different containers.

Ripe: Wine that is produced when the grapes have reached optimal ripeness.

Smoky: Wines with the aroma of smoke, char, fire, or burning. This might be due to the presence of soil on the grapes or char on the barrels used.

Sommelier: A wine butler or certified wine professional.

Smooth: When the wine feels soft and smooth against the roof of your mouth.

Spicy: When wines have the aroma of different spices, such as pepper, cinnamon, or cloves.

Sulfites: Preservatives used to improve the shelf life of wine.

Supple: These wines are young and lush.

Sweet: Wines that have a distinctive sweet aroma and taste.

Tannins: Compounds in wine that leave a bitter, dry feeling in the mouth.

Terroir: Influence of a vineyard's location on a wine's flavor.

Textured: A term used to describe how wine feels in the mouth.

Velvety: The wine has an opulent texture.

Vintner: Winemaker.

Woody: Wines that are reminiscent of the oak they were stored in. They smell of coffee, smoke, or vanilla and might have a dry taste. This is a winemaking flaw.

Yeast Nutrient: Additive used to support the activity of yeast during fermentation.

REFERENCES

A basic guide to malolactic fermentation in wine. (2021, June 7). MasterClass. https://www.masterclass.com/articles/a-basic-guide-to-malolactic-fermentation-in-wine

A guide to eye-catching wine labels. (n.d.). LabelNet. https://blog.labelnet.co.uk/blog/create-your-wine-labels

A quote by Andre Simon. (n.d.). GoodReads. https://www.goodreads.com/quotes/81870-wine-makes-every-meal-an-occasion-every-table-more-elegant

A quote by Galileo Galilei. (2022, May 12). GoodReads. https://www.goodreads.com/quotes/200391-wine-is-sunlight-held-together-by-water

A quote by Louis Pasteur. (2022, December 13). GoodReads https://www.goodreads.com/quotes/65187-wine-is-the-most-healthful-and-most-hygienic-of-beverages

Adamant, A. (2023, February 1). *Wine yeast: Choosing the right yeast for homemade wine (& mead).* Practical Self Reliance. https://practicalselfreliance.com/wine-yeast

Adaway, T. (2020, June 11). *10 ways the future of wine Is changing faster than you think.* Future Drinks Expo. https://www.linkedin.com/pulse/10-latest-innovations-winemaking-industry-tyrone-adaway-mba

Adeniyi, T. (2023, August 11). *23 best fruits for wine making.* A Soothing Food. https://asoothingfood.com/best-fruit-for-wine-making

Admin. (2012, July 6). *Pressing grapes.* Winemaker's Academy. https://winemakersacademy.com/pressing-grapes/

Admin. (2023, September 4). *Glossary of wine terminology.* Wine School. https://www.vinology.com/wine-terms

Admin–Blue Label. (2014, August 11). *5 ways to create a standout wine label.* Blue Label Packaging. https://www.bluelabelpackaging.com/blog/5-ways-to-create-a-standout-wine-label

Admin DVine. (2023, July 25). *The old and new worlds of wine: The differences.* DVine. https://www.d-vine.com/en/the-old-and-new-worlds-of-wine-the-differences

Adventures in Home Brewing. (n.d.). *Wine Making. Fermentation 101.* Adventures in Home Brewing. https://homebrewing.org/pages/wine-making-fermentation-101

Adventures in Home Brewing. (2019, November 18). *Basic wine making equipment list for beginners*. Adventures in Home Brewing. https://blog.homebrewing.org/basic-wine-making-equipment-list

Amerine, M. A. (2023, October 7). *Wine–aging and bottling*. Encyclopedia Britannica. https://www.britannica.com/topic/wine/Aging-and-bottling

Ando, A. (2022, September 19). *Top 10 fruits to make wine*. Honest Food Talks. https://www.honestfoodtalks.com/top-fruits-make-wine

Asimov, E. (2023, October 19). *The agony and ecstasy of home winemaking.* The New York Times. https://www.nytimes.com/2023/10/19/dining/drinks/home-wine-making.html

AWRI. (2012, September 29). *Yeast assimilable nitrogen (YAN).* The Australian Wine Research Institute. https://www.awri.com.au/industry_support/winemaking_resources/wine_fermentation/yan

AWRI. (2022, September 13). *Winemaking treatment–yeast choice.* The Australian Wine Research Institute. https://www.awri.com.au/industry_support/winemaking_resources/winemaking-practices/winemaking-treatment-yeast-choice/#:

Barrel hydration. (2018, July 8). NC Winery. https://www.ncwinery.com/barrel-hydration

Bartoletti, F. (2015, July 31). *Cleaning and sterilizing terracotta wine jar. Steam? Ozone or UV rays?* Artenova. https://jars.terracotta-artenova.com/cleaning-and-sanitizing-terracotta-wine-jar

Beard, J. (2013, January 16). *Top wine producing regions of the world.* Wine Folly. https://winefolly.com/lifestyle/top-wine-regions-of-the-world

Begg, R. (2023, October 13). *How to design a logo [step-by-step guide].* Hubspot Blog. https://blog.hubspot.com/marketing/how-to-design-logo

Beginner's home wine making checklist. (n.d.). Presque Isle Wine. https://www.piwine.com/beginner-winemakers-checklist.html

Benjamin Franklin quote: "The best investment is in the tools of one's own trade." (2019). Quotefancy. https://quotefancy.com/quote/772002/Benjamin-Franklin-The-best-investment-is-in-the-tools-of-one-s-own-trade

Berrigan, H. (2023, August 2). *Essential wine storage tips for fresh and flavorful bottles.* Vino Cheepo. https://vinocheepo.com/blogs/cheap-wine-blog/essential-wine-storage-tips-for-fresh-and-flavorful-bottles

Best wine quotes ever: Funny & classy wine. (2022, August 18). The Wine Cellar Group. https://www.thewinecellargroup.com/a-collection-of-the-best-wine-quotes-of-all-time

Blending to improve homemade wines. (n.d.). Adventures in Home Brewing. https://homebrewing.org/pages/blending-to-improve-homemade-wines

Blending wine with Pearson's Square. (2014, March 5). Winemaker's Academy. https://winemakersacademy.com/blending-wine-pearsons-square

Brainy Quote. (n.d.). *Joan Collins quotes*. Brainy Quote. https://www.brainyquote.com/quotes/joan_collins_386685

Braum, S. (n.d.). *Soil amendments for vineyards–what are the benefits?* Lodi Wine Growers. https://lodigrowers.com/soil-amendments-for-vineyards-what-are-the-benefits/#:

Brewsy Recipe Team. (2023, May 6). *What's the difference between primary and secondary fermentation?* Get Brewsy. https://getbrewsy.com/blogs/science/what-s-the-difference-between-primary-and-secondary-fermentation

Briscoe, S. (2023, May 8). *Basics: What does "microclimate" mean?* Wine Enthusiast. https://www.wineenthusiast.com/basics/drinks-terms-defined/microclimate-wine-definition

Bryan. (2016, February 18). *Top 10 reasons to make your own wine.* Great Fermentations. https://www.greatfermentations.com/top-10-reasons-to-make-your-own-wine

Buican, B.-C., et al. (2023). *"Orange" wine—the resurgence of an ancient winemaking technique: A review.* Agriculture, *13*(9), 1750. https://doi.org/10.3390/agriculture13091750

Burgess, L. (2016, August 22). *The crush Is the first step In turning grapes Into wine.* VinePair. https://vinepair.com/articles/the-crush-is-the-first-step-in-turning-grapes-into-wine

Burrows, R. (2020). *Vineyard world calendar.* SDSU Extension. https://extension.sdstate.edu/sites/default/files/2020-04/P-00153.pdf

Campbell, K. (2022, May 16). *Winery marketing: 11 ways to win more business.* C-Vent Blog. https://www.cvent.com/en/blog/hospitality/winery-marketing

Charest, R. (2019, May 16). *How sulfites affect a wine's chemistry.* SevenFifty Daily. https://daily.sevenfifty.com/how-sulfites-affect-a-wines-chemistry

Chase, A. (2019, March 22). *So you want to become a wine educator.* Grape Experience. https://www.grapeexperience.com/want-become-wine-educator-2

Choosing a wine cork. (n.d.) More Beer. https://www.morebeer.com/questions/235

Clarke, D. (2022, October 21). *7 types of wine fermenters (and their characteristics).* Letina. https://letina.com/en/blog/wine-fermenter-types

Clarke, S. (2023, May 4). *Winemaker groups promoting camaraderie and collaboration.* Wine Enthusiast. https://www.wineenthusiast.com/culture/wine/winemaker-groups-collaboration

Clemence, D. (2020, June 11). *Why does vineyard site location matter?* Philip Carter Winery. https://www.pcwinery.com/why-does-vineyard-site-location-matter

Climate, weather, and vineyard management. (2019, January 17). eVineyard. https://www.evineyardapp.com/blog/2019/01/17/climate-weather-and-vineyard-management

Club directory. (2023, March 28). WineMakerMag. https://winemakermag.com/resource/club-directory

Cole, G. (2023, March 23). *What you need to know about beverage alcohol licenses*. Avalara. https://www.avalara.com/blog/en/north-america/2023/03/beverage-alcohol-licenses-what-you-need-to-know.html

Cornwall, M. (2019, August 16). *4 laws you might have missed that are regulating the wine industry*. Copper Peak Logistics. https://copperpeaklogistics.com/4-laws-you-might-have-missed-that-are-regulating-the-wine-industry

Cox, A. (2023, September 4). *What is labelling? Definition, importance, types and more*. Triton Store. https://tritonstore.com.au/what-is-labelling

Cuber, J. (2020, December 2). *History of winemaking*. ArcGIS StoryMaps. https://storymaps.arcgis.com/stories/c5a01856223745d19ee5a2f640624b83

Cult Wine Investment. (2021, October 7). *What are the most common vineyard pests and diseases?* Cult Wine Investment. https://www.wineinvestment.com/learn/magazine/2021/10/what-are-the-most-common-vineyard-pests-and-diseases

Cult Wine Investment. (2021, June 28). *10 tech innovations that are changing the wine industry*. Cult Wines Investment. https://www.wineinvestment.com/learn/magazine/2021/06/10-tech-innovations-that-are-changing-the-wine-industry

Cyndi. (2020, February 26). *Keeping your vineyard free of pests and disease*. The Grapevine Magazine. https://thegrapevinemagazine.net/2020/02/keeping-your-vineyard-free-of-pests-and-disease/#:

D'Angelo, C. (2022, April 8). *How to write an authentic brand story*. Brandfolder. https://brandfolder.com/resources/how-to-write-brand-story

David A. (2016, October 7). *Which wine bottles for my homemade wine?* Danny's Wine & Beer Supplies. https://www.dannyswineandbeer.com/blogs/how-to/which-wine-bottles-for-my-homemade-wine

David A. (2021a, March 17). *7 easily-avoidable mistakes made by beginner winemakers*. Danny's Wine and Beer Supplies. https://www.dannyswineandbeer.com/blogs/how-to/easily-avoidable-mistakes-beginner-winemakers

Degassing wine. (n.d.). Winemakers Depot. https://www.winemakersdepot.com/Degassing-Wine?

Discover wines paired to your tastes. (2022). Good Pair Days. https://www.goodpairdays.com/guides/wine-regions/article/where-wine-grape-vines-grow-well/#:

Dominowski. (2016, February 18). *How to make wine at home: Troubleshooting problems with your wine*. The Lazy Winemaker. https://www.thelazywinemaker.com/how-to-make-wine-at-home-troubleshooting-problems-with-your-wine

Domoto, P. (2013). *Vineyard nutrition. Petiole/soil sample results are back, now what?* Kansas Grape Growers & Winemakers Association. https://www.prairiefirewinery.com/Cellar/wp-content/uploads/2016/12/Fertilizer-mgmt.2013-KS.pdf

E-40. (2013). *Ya Area*. Rick Rock. https://www.goodreads.com/quotes/210227-the-ultimate-goal-of-farming-is-not-the-growing-of

Eckstein, D. (2021, March 22). *Official playbook to the difference between white wine & red wine*. 7Cellars. https://www.7cellars.com/blogs/7cellars/official-playbook-to-the-difference-between-white-wine-red-wine#:

Editors. (2023, November 1). *Argon*. Encyclopedia Britannica. https://www.britan nica.com/science/argon-chemical-element

Effects of fermentation temperature on wine. (2013, October 30). Winemakers Academy. https://winemakersacademy.com/effects-fermentation-temperature-wine

8 essential wine making supplies beginners should own. (2021b, March 18). Danny's Wine & Beer. https://www.dannyswineandbeer.com/blogs/how-to/essential-wine-making-supplies

Eisenman, L. (n.d.-a). *Everything you wanted to know about wine yeasts*. Home Brew It. https://www.homebrewit.com/pages/everything-you-wanted-to-know-about-wine-yeasts

Eisenman, L. (n.d.-b). *Wine clarification and stabilization*. Genco Winemakers. https://www.gencowinemakers.com/docs/Wine%20Clarification%20and%20Stabilization.pdf

11 noteworthy wine storage tips to preserve wine quality. (2022, June 23). Storage Plus. https://www.storageplus.com.au/blog/11-noteworthy-wine-storage-tips-to-preserve-wine-quality#

Etham and District Winemakers Guild. (2021). *Winemakers guilds*. Amateur Wine. https://amateurwine.org.au/web-links#winemakers-guilds

Experimenting with wine: Why it's good for the soul. (2019, April 15). Winebuyers. https://www.winebuyers.com/en/blog/experimenting-with-wine-is-good-for-the-soul

Explore the world's top wine regions. (n.d.). Hillebrand Gori. https://www.hillebrand gori.com/media/publication/top-wine-regions-of-the-world

Explorer, W. (2023, March 14). *Wine bottles: How shape, size, and design affect your wine experience*. Bonner Private Wine Partnership. https://bonnerprivatewines.com/the-wine-explorers-letter/bottle-shapes-what-do-they-mean

Fact sheet–Achieving successful malolactic fermentation. (September 2020). Australian Wine Research Institute. https://www.awri.com.au/wp-content/uploads/2011/06/Malolactic-fermentation.pdf

5 pioneering female winemakers who shook up the wine world. (2021, March 7). Bright Cellars. https://www.brightcellars.com/blogs/learn/5-pioneering-female-wine makers-who-shook-up-the-wine-world

5 things to know before shipping wine abroad. (2023, February 28). Vignoble Export. https://www.vignoblexport.com/ship-wine-to-foreign

Flat–slope vineyards. (n.d.). Grape to Glass. https://grape-to-glass.com/index.php/flat-slope-vineyards/#:

Food & Wine Editors. (n.d.). *15 rules for great wine and food pairings.* Food & Wine Magazine. https://www.foodandwine.com/food-and-wine-pairing-guide-6409590

Fragiacomo, L. (n.d.). *Flavor profiles of wine for beginners.* Alkypal. https://alkypal.com.au/wine/flavour-profiles-of-wine.html#:

Fucuoka, M. (2022, September 10). *A quote from The One-Straw Revolution.* GoodReads. https://www.goodreads.com/quotes/210227-the-ultimate-goal-of-farming-is-not-the-growing-of

Furrow, D. (2018, February 28). *Hemingway really understood wine.* Exploring the Philosophy of Food and Wine. https://foodandwineaesthetics.com/2018/02/28/hemingway-really-understood-wine

Garnet, S., & Read, P. E. (n.d.). *Trellis systems for your vineyard.* Viticulture. https://viticulture.unl.edu/trellis-systems

Goldammer, T. (2021). *Grape grower's handbook: A guide to viticulture for wine production.* Apex Publishers. https://www.wine-grape-growing.com/wine_grape_growing/vineyard_site_selection/vineyard_site_selection_topography.htm

Goldhawke, B. (2022, May 13). *5 ways to reduce wine oxidation.* Cellar Data. https://www.barrelwise.ca/blog/5-ways-to-reduce-wine-oxidation

Goode, J. (n.d.). *Struggling vines produce better wines.* Wine Anorak. https://www.wineanorak.com/struggle.htm

Greguit, P. (2023, May 5). *Basics: The dos and don'ts of wine labels.* Wine Enthusiast. https://www.wineenthusiast.com/culture/wine/wine-labels-good-bad/

Hagan, M. (2020a, April 28). *Wine terms to help you sound like an expert.* Usual. https://usualwines.com/blogs/knowledge-base/wine-terms

Hagan, M. (2020b, October 13). *A curious and captivating history of wine.* Usual. https://usualwines.com/blogs/knowledge-base/history-of-wine

Haibach, R. (2017, June 26). *Basic home winemaking equipment.* Home Winemaking. https://www.smartwinemaking.com/post/basic-winemaking-equipment

Haibach, R. (2019, December 23). *Managing sulfites in wine.* Smart Winemaking. https://www.smartwinemaking.com/post/managing-sulfites-in-wine

Hakim, S. (2018). *Diversity of wine yeasts.* UC Davis Viticulture & Enology. https://wineserver.ucdavis.edu/industry-info/enology/wine-microbiology/yeast-mold/diversity-wine-yeasts

Hansen, M. (2011, April 1). *When do grapevines need irrigation?* Good Fruit Grower. https://www.goodfruit.com/when-do-grapevines-need-irrigation/

Hansen, S. (n.d.). *Homemade wine vs. commercial: 4 important differences.* Home Brew Advice. https://homebrewadvice.com/homemade-wine-vs-commercial

Heimoff, S. (2015, March 20). *Why is blending wine important?* La Crema. https://www.lacrema.com/blending-wine-important/

Hill, K. (2023, April 25). *60 brilliant wine quotes that'll suit your taste buds*. Quotement. https://quotement.com/wine-quotes

Hirst, K. (2019, November 25). *What genius culture first thought of fermenting grapes?* ThoughtCo. https://www.thoughtco.com/wine-origins-archaeology-and-history-173240

History of wine South Africa. (n.d.). Winebow. https://www.winebow.com/knowledge/wine/south-africa

How does geography affect a wine's style? (2021, August 24). WSET Global. https://www.wsetglobal.com/knowledge-centre/blog/2021/august/24/how-does-geography-affect-a-wine-s-style

How does location affect a wine's taste? A terroir tour! (2021, February 8). Science Wanders. https://www.sciencewanders.com/how-does-location-affect-a-wines-taste-a-terroir-tour

How does temperature affect fermentation? (2023, June 20). Atlas Scientific. https://atlas-scientific.com/blog/how-does-temperature-affect-fermentation

How long do primary and secondary fermentations last? (2014, May 30). Winemakers Academy. https://winemakersacademy.com/long-primary-secondary-fermentations

How to become a sommelier: Tips and tricks for breaking into the industry. (2019, August 20). MasterClass. https://www.masterclass.com/articles/what-is-a-sommelier

How to become a wine educator. (2021, February 9). WSET Global. https://www.wsetglobal.com/knowledge-centre/blog/2021/february/09/how-to-become-a-wine-educator

How to export wine. (2022, May 7). iContainers. https://www.icontainers.com/export/how-to-export-wine

How to make your own wine gift basket. (2022, January 19). Marketview Liquor. https://www.marketviewliquor.com/blog/how-to-make-your-own-wine-gift-basket

How to store wine at home: 7 tips. (2021, August 4). MasterClass. https://www.masterclass.com/articles/how-to-properly-store-wine-at-home

How to taste and assess wine. (2023). Firstleaf. https://www.firstleaf.com/wine-school/article/how-to-taste-wine-and-assess-wine

How to taste wine and understand your palate: A guide to navigating a wine tasting. (2021, July 30). MasterClass. https://www.masterclass.com/articles/how-to-taste-wine-and-understand-your-palate-a-guide-to-navigating-a-wine-tasting

How to taste wine. (2023, March 10). Virgin Wines. https://www.virginwines.co.uk/hub/wine-guide/wine-basics/how-to-taste-wine

Indeed Editorial Team. (2022, October 1). *How to become a winemaker: Definition, steps and FAQ*. Indeed Career Guide. https://www.indeed.com/career-advice/finding-a-job/how-to-become-wine-maker

Irrigation in viticulture. (2023, July 23). Wikipedia. https://en.wikipedia.org/wiki/Irrigation_in_viticulture

IWCA. (n.d.). *International wineries for climate action.* International Wineries for Climate Action. https://www.iwcawine.org

Judy R. (2017, August 24). *Trellising systems in the vineyard–What are they and why are they used.* Uncorked. https://www.cawineclub.com/blog/what-are-vineyard-trellising-systems-why-are-they-important

Kanner, E. (2023, April 24). *How old school grape crushing by foot makes better wine.* Alcohol Professor. https://www.alcoholprofessor.com/blog-posts/grape-crushing-by-foot-better-wine

Kebler, D. C. (2023, April 6). *Different types of wine presses and their uses.* Sraml. https://sraml.com/different-types-of-wine-presses-and-their-uses/#:~

Keyser, R. (2018, September 1). *The importance of wine storage.* Vinum 55. https://www.vinum55.com/importance-wine-storage

Klodd, A., & Rosen, C. (2021). *Tissue and soil nutrient testing for cold climate grapes.* University of Minnesota Extension. https://extension.umn.edu/commercial-fruit-growing-guides/tissue-and-soil-nutrient-testing-cold-climate-grapes#guidelines-for-taking-soil-samples-in-vineyards-2666210

Kraus, E. (2017, August 19). *What's the difference between crushing and pressing grapes?* Adventures in Homebrewing. https://blog.homebrewing.org/difference-crushing-pressing-grapes

Kraus, E. (2019, October 16). *To airlock or not to airlock during primary fermentation.* Adventures in Homebrewing. https://blog.homebrewing.org/air-lock-primary-fermentation

Kraus, E. (2022a, July 21). *Adding oak chips during fermentation.* Adventures in Home Brewing. https://blog.homebrewing.org/adding-oak-chips-during-fermentation-after-fermentation/#:

Kraus, E. (2022b, August 1). *When to start secondary fermentation.* Adventures in Home Brewing. https://blog.homebrewing.org/when-to-start-secondary-fermentation-wine

Kraus, E. (2022c, August 11). *Buying corks for wine bottles.* Adventures in Home Brewing. https://blog.homebrewing.org/buying-corks-for-wine-bottles

Kuhlken, J. (2018, October 24). *The art and science of blending to achieve complexity in wine.* Pedernales Cellars. https://www.pedernalescellars.com/blog/The-Art-and-Science-of-Blending-to-Achieve-Complexity-in-Wine

Kuniswa, E. (2022, June 17). *6 proven wine marketing strategies [+ bonus tools].* Grappos. https://www.grappos.com/blog/6-proven-wine-marketing-strategies

Leonardo da Vinci Quote: "The discovery of a good wine is increasingly better for mankind

than the discovery of a new star." (n.d.). Quotefancy. https://quotefancy.com/quote/852620/Leonardo-da-Vinci-The-discovery-of-a-good-wine-is-increasingly-better-for-mankind-than

Leve, J. (2018, March 4). *Wine glossary of terms.* The Wine Cellar Insider. https://www.thewinecellarinsider.com/wine-topics/wine-educational-questions/abc-of-wine-glossary-of-wine-terms

Martellotto, G. (2022, January 12). *Everything you wanted to know about aging wine.* Big Hammer Wines. https://www.bighammerwines.com/blogs/news/everything-you-wanted-to-know-about-aging-wine

Michael Broadbent quote: "Drinking good wine with good food in good company is one of life's most civilized pleasures." (n.d.). Quotefancy. https://quotefancy.com/quote/1607884/Michael-Broadbent-Drinking-good-wine-with-good-food-in-good-company-is-one-of-life-s-most

Michelman, J. (2021, May 20). *You should absolutely age your own wine. Here's how to do it.* Eater. https://www.eater.com/22442472/guide-to-aging-wine-best-bottles-to-age

Microclimates and their pivotal role in viticulture. (2023, September 7). Vinetur. https://www.vinetur.com/en/2023090775158/microclimates-and-their-pivotal-role-in-viticulture.html

Moore, V. (2023, November 14). *How to taste wine.* BBC Good Food. https://www.bbcgoodfood.com/howto/guide/how-to-taste-wine

Mowery, L. (2023, May 4). *Basics: Wine faults and how to recognize them.* Wine Enthusiast. Wine Enthusiast. https://www.wineenthusiast.com/basics/wine-faults

Oak barrels and containers: learn about the different options. (2021, January 27). Agrovin. https://agrovin.com/en/oak-barrels-and-containers-learn-about-the-different-options

Oak barrel care guide. (2012, September 5). More Wine. https://morewinemaking.com/articles/Oak_barrel_care_guide

O'Donnell, D. (2022, November 27). *The importance of pH in wine making.* Sensorex. https://sensorex.com/ph-wine-making

Owczarek, A. (2019, April 2). *All you need to know about designing wine labels.* Packhelp. https://packhelp.com/wine-label-design

Ozturk, E., et al. (2023). Message in a bottle: An exploratory study on the role of wine-bottle design in capturing consumer attention. *Beverages*, 9(2), 36. https://doi.org/10.3390/beverages9020036

Pambianchi, D. (2019, October 1). *Choosing a wine yeast strain.* WineMaker Magazine. https://winemakermag.com/technique/1073-choosing-a-yeast-strain-techniques

Panel., E. (2022, November 17). *15 essential aspects of any successful brand.* Forbes.

https://www.forbes.com/sites/forbesbusinesscouncil/2022/11/17/15-essential-aspects-of-any-successful-brand/?sh=6e6f2785558a

Patterson, L. (2023, August 18). *How to design a stunning wine label.* Sttark. https://www.sttark.com/blog/how-to-design-a-stunning-wine-label

Pressing a red wine fermentation. (2012, February 22). More Winemaking. https://morewinemaking.com/articles/pressing_red_wine

Proverbs about drink. (n.d.). List of Proverbs. https://www.listofproverbs.com/keywords/drink

Pruning, the most critical activity we do in the vineyard each year. (n.d.). Hayes Family Wines. https://www.hayesfamilywines.com/blog/pruning

Publications Checkout. (2017, July 6). *Terrible labels, great wine: Six superb bottles hurt by bad art.* Hospitality Ireland. https://www.hospitalityireland.com/drinks/terrible-labels-great-wine-six-superb-bottles-hurt-bad-art-45869

Puckett, M. (2016, March 20). *9 steps to becoming a wine expert.* Wine Folly. https://winefolly.com/deep-dive/becoming-a-wine-expert

Puckette M. (2021, November 9.) *What is malolactic fermentation? The buttery taste in wine.* Wine Folly. https://winefolly.com/deep-dive/what-is-malolactic-fermentation-the-buttery-taste-in-wine

Raspuzzi, D. (2018, June 14). *Sourcing grapes.* WineMakers Magazine. https://winemakermag.com/article/sourcing-grapes

Rawat, A. (2022, March 15). *The art of blending wines–the famous wine blends.* Sommelier Business. https://sommelierbusiness.com/en/articles/insights-1/the-art-of-blending-wines-the-famous-wine-blends-310.htm

Romano, J. (2022, December 25). *How to create a compelling brand story.* Wix Blog. https://www.wix.com/blog/brand-story

Roncoroni, J., et al. (2015, July). *Weed management in organic vineyards–Grape agriculture: Pest management guidelines.* University of California. https://ipm.ucanr.edu/agriculture/grape/weed-management-in-organic-vineyards

Rosen, C. (2014). *Soil fertility for wine grapes.* University of Minnesota Extension. https://www.canr.msu.edu/uploads/234/43701/1_Intro_grape_soil_fertility_rosen_2.pdf

Russell, C. (2019, February 13). *How does wine fermentation work?* 2Hawk Vineyard & Winery. https://www.2hawk.wine/2019/02/13/how-does-wine-fermentation-work/

Serpo, K. (2023, June 6). *Explore wine flavors: Ultimate guide to wine flavor profiles.* The Wine Club Philippines. https://wineclub.ph/wine-flavor-profiles

Shafer, E. (2023, September 12). *Home winemaking the right way.* Mother Earth News. https://www.motherearthnews.com/real-food/home-wine-making-zmaz95djzjma/#:

Shallenberger, N. (2016, September 16). *How to create the best red wine blend*—a *lesson at four brix winery*. Uncorked. https://www.cawineclub.com/blog/how-to-create-best-red-wine-blend/

Shoemaker, J. (2020, August 3). *Your best crush and press*. WineMaker Magazine. https://winemakermag.com/article/crush-press-2

Shoemaker, S. & Petre, A. (2022, April 12). *What is BPA? Should I be concerned about it?* Healthline. https://www.healthline.com/nutrition/what-is-bpa#Potential-health-effects-of-BPA-exposure

Shumaker, R. (2020, October 22). *15 of the most effective wine marketing tactics*. Sfgate. https://marketing.sfgate.com/blog/15-of-the-most-effective-wine-marketing-tactics

Simon. (n.d.). *All fermentation vessels you can use at home*. Home Brew Advice. https://homebrewadvice.com/fermentation-vessels-you-can-use-at-home

Spencer, B. (2010, December 25). *Aging wine—an odyssey of containers*. Into Wine. https://www.intowine.com/aging-wine-%E2%80%93-odyssey-containers

Stevenson, R. L. (n.d.). *Robert Louis Stevenson quotes*. Brainy Quotes. https://www.brainyquote.com/quotes/robert_louis_stevenson_155195

Strafne, Er. (2019, June 20). *Vineyard site selection*. Mississippi State University. https://grapes.extension.org/vineyard-site-selection

Sonoma Cast Stone. (2018, April 10). *Care and maintenance for your concrete tank*. Concrete Wine Tanks. https://www.concretewinetanks.com/downloads/cwt_cm.pdf

Sulfur stick. (n.d.). Northeast Winemaking. https://northeastwinemaking.com/products/sulfur-stick#:

Sullivan, S. P. (2023, May 4). *Basics: The why, when and how of wine blending*. Wine Enthusiast. https://www.wineenthusiast.com/culture/wine/wine-blending

Svilane, L. (2023, May 8). *Why is wine stored in glass?* Friends of Glass. https://www.friendsofglass.com/taste/why-is-wine-stored-in-glass/#:

Tanner, A. (n.d.). *Wine subscriptions paired to your tastes*. Good Pair Days. https://www.goodpairdays.com/guides/wine-101/article/wine-bottle-shapes/#:

Tarrier, E. (2022, May 20). *7 simple steps to host a wine tasting at home*. Visit Prosecco Italy. https://visitproseccoitaly.com/how-to-host-a-wine-tasting-at-home

10 ways the future of wine Is changing faster than you think. (2021, September 1). Future Drinks Expo. https://futuredrinksexpo.com/en/blog/insights-64/10-ways-the-future-of-wine-is-changing-faster-than-you-think-255.htm

Terrazas, A. (2021, March 16). *Wine & weather: The best climate for grapes*. Palate Club. https://www.palateclub.com/climate-for-grapes

Thach, D. L., & MW. (2013, August 29). *What are the major cool and warm climate grape varietals?* Dr. Liz Thach, MW. https://lizthachmw.com/winestars/what-are-the-major-cool-and-warm-climate-wine-varietals

The 5 best experience gifts for wine lovers (2022 edition). (2023, November 12). Amazing

Co. https://www2.amazingco.me/blog/best-5-experience-gifts-for-wine-lovers-2023

The best wine regions in the world. (n.d.). First Leaf. https://www.firstleaf.com/wine-school/article/top-wine-regions

The difference between primary and secondary fermentation. (2013, May 30). Winemakers Academy. https://winemakersacademy.com/secondary-fermentation

The history of South African wine. (2021, October 7). Which Wine Farm. https://whichwinefarm.co.za/the-history-of-south-african-wine

The role of barrels and vats in making wine. (2016, April 14). Gourmet Odyssey. https://www.gourmetodyssey.com/blog/2016/04/14/231-The-role-of-vats-barrels-and-other-types-of-container-in-making-wine

The role of yeast in winemaking. (2023, April 21). Grapeworks. https://grapeworks.com.au/news/winemaking/the-role-of-yeast-in-winemaking

The wine explorer's letter. (2023, March 14). Bonners Private Wines. https://bonnerprivatewines.com/the-wine-explorers-letter/bottle-shapes-what-do-they-mean

Time, D. (2015, December 10). *Common craft winemaking mistakes (and how to avoid them!).* RJS Craft Winemaking. https://www.rjscraftwinemaking.com/craft-and-cork/the-most-common-craft-winemaking-mistakes-and-how-to-avoid-them/#:

Tips for making wine with fruits other than grapes. (2023, March 1). Lompoc Wine Factory. https://lompocwinefactory.com/wine-with-fruits-other-than-grapes

Top 4 occasions to give a homemade wine and still have some left for you. (2017, March 22). VinBon. https://www.vinbon.com/top-5-occasions-to-give-a-homemade-wine-and-still-have-some-left-for-you

Troubleshooting common winemaking problems. (n.d.). Northeast Winemaking. https://northeastwinemaking.com/pages/troubleshooting-common-winemaking-problems

Tutorial on wine making—Lesson 4 of 6. (n.d.) Winemaker's Depot. https://winemakersdepot.com/Tutorial-on-Wine-Making-Lesson-4-of-6

Vineyard soil sampling guidelines. (2018, October 3). eVineyard. https://www.evineyardapp.com/blog/2018/10/03/vineyards-soil-sampling-guidelines

Vinolove. (2020, January 30). *What is the difference between white and red wine production?* Wine Tasting and Tour. https://www.vinolove.club/proizvodstvobelogoikrasnogovina

Wallace, K. (2020, November 21). *The 10 absolute best wine regions in the world.* Wine School. https://www.vinology.com/wine-regions-world

Waterhouse, A. (2015, February 4). *A chemist explains why corks matter when storing wine.* Wine Folly. https://winefolly.com/deep-dive/chemist-explains-corks-matter-storing-wine

Watson, J. (2011, January 24). *Stirring during primary fermentation*. Winemaking Talk. https://www.winemakingtalk.com/threads/stirring-during-primary-fermentation.11816

Weatherwax, J. (n.d.). *Does wine age in the bottle | Does wine get better with age?* Binwise. https://home.binwise.com/blog/wine-better-age

Wenz, K. (2023, May 23). *No regrets: Discovering the world of wine as a second career.* Vintner Project. https://vintnerproject.com/wine/no-regrets-discovering-the-world-of-wine-as-a-second-career

What does John 2:10 mean? (n.d.). Bible Ref. https://www.bibleref.com/John/2/John-2-10.html

What is a Brix refractometer, and how do they work? (2020, October 6). Instrument Choice. https://www.instrumentchoice.com.au/news/what-is-a-brix-refractometer-and-how-do-they-work

Why proper wine storage is important. (2011, November 16). Ideal55. https://ideal55.com/why-proper-wine-storage-is-important

Wine bottles: The importance of glass color for wine. (2020, April 28). Gravity Wine House. https://gravitywinehouse.com/blog/wine-bottle-glass-color

Wine faults series. (2020). Iowa State University Extension. https://store.extension.iastate.edu/product/15980

Winemaking facts and myths (n.d.). Brewery Lane. https://brewerylane.com/wine/winemaking-facts-myths

Wine quotes. (n.d.). Ceja Vineyards.https://www.cejavineyards.com/Wine-Quotes

Wikipedia Contributors. (2023, November 8). *Clarification and stabilization of wine.* Wikipedia. https://en.wikipedia.org/wiki/Clarification_and_stabilization_of_wine

Wilson, S. J. (2022, September 15). *What makes a brand successful?* Steven J. Wilson. https://stevenjwilson.com/what-makes-a-brand-successful/#:

Wine Country Collective. (2022, August 26). *What is crush in wine country? We'll tell you.* Wine Country. https://www.winecountry.com/blog/what-is-crush/

Wine International Association WIA. (n.d.). Wine International Association. https://wineinternationalassociation.org

Winemaking frequently asked questions. (n.d.). Northeast Winemaking. https://northeastwinemaking.com/pages/faq

Wine marketing: 16 steps to vine growth & marketing success. (n.d.). Binwise. https://home.binwise.com/blog/wine-marketing

Wine pairing tips for beginners. (2021, June 17). The Wine Cellar Group. https://www.thewinecellargroup.com/wine-pairing-tips-for-beginners

Winery marketing tips to grow more business. (2022, September 23). Sommeliers Choice Awards. https://sommelierschoiceawards.com/en/blog/insights-1/winery-marketing-tips-to-grow-more-business-690.htm

WineSHP Crush. (n.d.). University of Washington School of Public Health. https://depts.washington.edu/wineryhs/Crush.html#:

Wynne, J. (n.d.). *The history of wine.* Arena Flowers. https://www.arenaflowers.com/pages/history-of-wine

Yeast strains chart. (2020, November 19). WineMaking Magazine. https://winemakermag.com/resource/yeast-strains-chart

Young, B. (2018, February 23). *How to prune grapevines: Vineyard farming for winemaking.* Jordan Winery. https://www.jordanwinery.com/blog/how-to-prune-grape-vines

Zebra ZSB. (n.d.). *How to brand with eye-catching wine labels.* Zebra Technologies. https://www.zebra.com/smb/gb/en/Blog/how-many-people-are-really-seeing-and-tasting-your-wine.html

Zhang, A. (n.d.). *How to become a wine connoisseur (15 useful tips).* Vinovest. https://www.vinovest.co/blog/wine-connoisseur

Printed in Great Britain
by Amazon

46657250R00148